Praise for *Teach! The Art of Teaching Adults*

Your textbook *Teach!* should be read by all directors of education and teachers from all sectors of education. The text is straight-forward and easy to follow. Meyer gives us a step-by-step method for teachers to learn to monitor their effectiveness, relate to the student and to assess knowledge with a variety of methods.

Lynda L. Wheeler
Director of Education, California College

After taking a series of classes at a major university in educational philosophy, learning theory, classroom management and curriculum development I then read *Teach!* by Leo A. Meyer. *Teach!* sums up everything I really needed to know in order to effectively deliver quality instruction. Mr. Meyer has distilled what every instructor really needs to know to become an excellent instructor in this book and makes it plain and easy to understand.

Norm Christopherson
Senior Training Specialist, York International UPG

We have spent thousands of dollars in Instructor Education over the last several years, but the best money we have ever spent was purchasing the *Teach* book by Leo Meyer. It is the most concise and well-written book about teaching I have ever seen. It is geared to our needs at our electrical apprenticeship and covers the same material that you can pay thousands of dollars for in seminars. I highly recommend this inexpensive way to train your instructors on how to teach students effectively.

Mel Switzer
Assistant Training Director, Alameda County Electrical JATC

I have been an HVAC-R instructor since 1968. I have numerous vocational courses, and have earned a 'Master Degree in Vocational Education.'

After many costly text books and courses taken through this process. I finally discovered *Teach* by Leo A. Meyer. This could have been a god-send if I had only had this book to learn from at the beginning of my teaching career, as well as to train and assist instructors that I have trained over the years.

I would like to recommend this book for new instructors/teachers as well as seasoned instructors/teachers in HVAC-R. The *Teach* book is easily adaptable for any vocational subject.

Thank you for this wonderful work.

Richard Jones,
HVAC-R Coordinator
Arizona Automotive Institute

Mel Switzer, of the electrical JATC, asked me to email you about my experience with the *Teach!* book. I have found it helpful both in its author's real world experience and as a way to organize my lesson presentation. I use the lesson plan form to map out my lecture, lab and interactive activities. The book was also shared with a friend of mine who teaches auto mechanics. He was skeptical when the book was given, but commended the author's practical and well rounded approach. Thank you for publishing this book.

Dan Holgate
Inspector, UC Berkeley

The Academics want us to think teaching is complicated and intricate. It's not—and your book presents teaching it its proper context. My favorites (the 3 F's and Tricks of the Trade) are great examples. Granted, we train in the field of Cosmetology, not physics, but it's the techniques, not the subject matter that counts. Thank you for your ability to present teaching as it should be… plain and simple.

Alan Cox
Director, Hayward College of Cosmetology

Teach! is just what all of our instructors and apprenticeship coordinators have been looking for over the years to help them in their apprenticeship training classes. It lays out, in an easy-to-understand format, suggestions on how instructors can help make their classes more interesting, boost attentiveness in class, and in general help their apprentices to better learn what's being presented in lesson plans.

There is no doubt that Leo Meyer's experiences as an instructor are the contributing factors as to why this is such a valuable teaching tool, and why it is easy to understand.

You have created something here which needs to be read by anyone who finds themselves in a teaching/classroom setting. You have made the jobs of our instructors and coordinators a lot easier with this book. They all loved it.

Robert J. Krul
Apprenticeship Coordinator,
United Union of Roofers, Waterproofers and Allied Workers

Teach!
THE ART OF TEACHING ADULTS

Leo A. Meyer

2nd Edition

LAMA Books
www.lamabooks.com

LAMA Books
2381 Sleepy Hollow Ave.
Hayward CA 94545-3429
888-452-6244 • 510-785-1099 Fax
lama@lamabooks.com • www.lamabooks.com

ISBN 978-0-88069-037-9
ISBN 0-88069-037-2
© Copyright 2005 by LAMA Books

All rights reserved. Printed in the United States of America. No part of this publication may be reproduced, stored in a retrieval system, or transmitted in any form or by any means—electronic, mechanical, photocopying, recording, or otherwise—without the written permission of the publisher.

TABLE OF CONTENTS

BEFORE YOU START

For my first teaching job, a school administrator called me at work and asked, "Will you teach a night class for us?" When I said yes, he responded, "Okay, you start next Tuesday night at seven."

That was my preparation for teaching—a trial by fire. Many mistakes later, I found out what I should have known before I entered that first classroom. The ideas in this book were developed through the experience of many years of night school, high school, community college teaching, and school administration—plus many teacher training classes both as a student and instructor.

This book is about practical teaching methods that work. It has been a valuable resource in a variety of teaching situations—business, industrial, educational, professional, and informal settings.

With this book I give you the knowledge that I wish I had possessed at the start of my first class. I know it will make your teaching easier and more rewarding. But the greatest reason for this book is to ensure that students do not have to endure the inept teaching that my first students suffered through while I learned at their expense.

Chapter 1

FIRST THINGS FIRST

Teaching can be rewarding or frustrating depending on how you teach.

It is something of an art—every teacher does it partly by intuition, partly by personality. But there are specific techniques that let you apply your art effectively. Follow these tips and you will have the most rewarding experience of all—seeing your skills and knowledge multiplied in the many students who learn from you.

If you have never taught before, this book can prepare you to meet your first class confidently and competently. If you already have some teaching experience, it will help you polish your skills and provide you with some fresh ideas and insights. I have taught many kinds of classes in occupational and industrial skills over the years—including high school, apprenticeship, in-service, college, and teacher training classes. I hope my experience can feed into your teaching.

You may be teaching occasional classes for new workers who need to learn new skills quickly. You may be a supervisor, teaching more advanced skills to employees with a varying range of experience. Perhaps you are an apprentice instructor at the local community college in a classroom with a shop attached. You may teach safety and job skills in tailgate sessions that are very informal. Or, you may be teaching a group of 18-year-old new hires.

Whatever your situation, the same basic principles of teaching will help you do the job right. Some of the nuts and bolts advice applies to some situations but not all. Take what you can use in your particular situation.

CONDITIONS FOR LEARNING

We still don't know exactly what takes place in the brain when we learn. Apparently we develop new nerve paths and nerve connections as electrical impulses zap around, but how it happens isn't clear.

Fortunately, we know something far more important about learning—we know the **conditions** we have to create to make learning happen. As a teacher, you should do more than dispense knowledge. You must create conditions that allow you to teach as much as you can and allow your students to learn as much as they can.

There are three kinds of conditions you must create or manage in a class:

- Conditions the student brings to class

- Conditions you set up before class

- Conditions you create in class

CONDITIONS THE STUDENT BRINGS TO CLASS

Your students bring their own conditions for learning with them:

- Motivation

- Ability

- Attitude

Some of this you can't do anything about; you simply have to work with what you have. But some can be changed if you work at it.

Motivation

Motivation is probably the most important condition for learning. If someone isn't ready to learn, there is no way you can make them learn.

However, you can motivate most students to learn. Later chapters will give you specific ways to motivate your students. You have to learn to deal with two kinds of motivation—willingness to learn a particular lesson and willingness to master the course in general.

Your students may be in your class because their job requires it. Attitudes can range from "I'm here because I have to be and I dare you to teach me anything" to "I want to be the best technician there is—teach me everything **now!**" In job-related classes, most workers can see the connection between what they learn and what they will earn, so they are ready and eager to learn. However, some of them are there only because they want to hold their job, and they clearly resent having to be there. Most of them are somewhere between the totally turned on and the totally turned off. You have to learn to deal with the whole range of attitudes.

Ability

Ability to learn is almost as important as motivation. However, a student with limited ability but plenty of motivation and determination will often out-perform the genius with a bad attitude. Ability counts for a lot, but motivation can be the most critical factor.

Some students may be limited by their intellectual ability. That's something you can't change, but at least you can motivate them to do the best they can. You have to settle for the goal of taking them as far as possible—which is always farther than the place they started from.

Some may be limited by a lack of basic skills, such as the ability to read or do arithmetic. This is not the same as the lack of ability to learn. There are many reasons why someone who did not learn in the lower grades may be able to master the basic skills now as an adult. They may be able to catch up in a fairly short time now that they are more mature.

If some of your students lack the basic skills, try to get them into remedial classes that will give them the needed skills. You probably can't do much about it in your own class. You can't take too much time from the whole class to devote to one person. Besides, someone with learning deficiencies has experienced failure for twelve years of schooling. It will take an expert to remedy the situation now.

However, you can motivate the student to get some help, and you can find remedial classes. Contact your local school district, community college, or library to find out what is available in your community for adults who need help.

Attitude

Your students are a mixed bag—they have different combinations of abilities and attitudes, and they will have different reactions to you. With some, being a friend and listener will change their attitude. For others, being a tough (but fair) drill sergeant will work better. Your course of action with any individual is something that you have to decide according to your instincts and experience.

If someone in your class is having trouble, try to find out if there are some overwhelming problems outside of class such as family problems, drugs, or finances. Some of these you may be able to help solve and some you cannot. But if you at least recognize the problem, you will be more understanding and patient.

CONDITIONS YOU SET UP BEFORE CLASS

Before the class starts, set up the conditions that will make it work:

- Set clear goals
- Have teaching materials on hand
- Plan short steps of learning
- Schedule enough time

Set Clear Goals

Create clear, reasonable goals for your class. You have to know exactly what you are going to teach. Even more important, your students need to know exactly what they are expected to learn, so they need to see a written list of clear goals.

Often, students perform poorly because they don't understand what's expected of them. They get discouraged and lose their motivation. If you give your class a clear set of goals at the beginning of each class, they can focus on what they need to know.

Make sure your list of goals is reasonable. It's very easy to plan way too much for one session. A process or project that seems easy to you might be quite demanding and difficult for your students. Set your goals with a novice in mind, and limit them to a reasonable list that you can really cover well in one lesson.

Chapter 6 will show you how to put together a good set of goals—not too little and not too much.

Have Teaching Materials On Hand

Be prepared. Have all your teaching materials organized and available to keep the class moving along smoothly. Teaching materials can be classroom equipment, such as chalkboards and overhead projectors, or lab equipment, such as the tools and supplies you need for demonstrations.

Nothing makes a teacher look worse than not having the tools of the trade at hand. If you have to stop class to hunt down a piece of chalk or if you have to stop a demonstration because you misplaced your tools or instruments, you will look incompetent and you will lose control of your class.

At the very least, not having all your tools ready means lost time while you hunt them down or make do with a substitute. That means the class has less time to learn. Even worse, an unnecessary break in your presentation will disrupt their concentration and focus. If you lose control of the class for even a few minutes, it takes much longer than that for you to get them focused on work again.

If you have to fumble around for missing equipment too often, your trainees will lose respect for you as a teacher. Even reluctant students admire a competent, efficient teacher. You have to be a good craftsman as a teacher just as you are a good craftsman on the job. That means having the right materials—where you need them and when you need them.

The best guarantee for having all the learning tools available is to have a clear lesson plan with a list of all the tools and materials you need. A later chapter will show you how to prepare a lesson plan that will keep your class running smoothly.

Plan Short Steps of Learning

Your students are bound to succeed if you move them along with a sequence of short, manageable steps. One short step leads to another and another. Success builds upon success. If you give them too much all at once, they get confused and discouraged—and failure builds upon failure.

Most likely, you know very well the material you are teaching. It all seems easy to you. It's not always easy to look at it from the beginner's point of view, but you must. Plan carefully so that you give them only as much as they can absorb and retain in a single lesson.

Suppose you teach plastering, and on the first day of class you tell your students, "Here's a stud wall—put on the lath and plaster the wall." They won't know where or how to start, and the job will seem impossible.

Suppose you are more reasonable and explain the whole process of how to put on the lath and plaster. This time the student has some idea of what to do but will probably forget some steps and get confused about others. The job will be a failure.

On the other hand, you could break the same job into a number of small steps:

- Using plastering tools
- Applying lath
- Applying mortar with a hawk and trowel
- Applying a scratch coat
- Applying dots and screeds
- Using the darby and slicker
- Applying a finish coat

You teach each step thoroughly, making sure that the student understands each one and masters each skill before going on to the next. The final job is a success.

Small steps add up to big accomplishments. They create success all around: your class will be successful at mastering their skills and you will be successful at turning out workers who really know their trade.

Schedule Enough Time

Every new skill takes a certain amount of time to master. So give your class enough time to learn. Not everything can be learned in a single session, and one time through won't make anyone an expert.

Think of how you mastered the skills you have. Most of them were acquired over some length of time. For one thing, most of us can practice a hand skill for only a short time before interest and energy lag. It also takes time for hand and mind to coordinate in a new hand skill.

This is obvious if you think of gaining a complex hand skill like playing the piano. If you practiced 60 hours in one week, you would gain some skill. However, if you spread those same 60 hours of practice over one hour a day for two months, you would gain much more skill with the same investment of time.

Individual pace is something every teacher understands from seeing some students take twice as long as others doing the same job. Everyone learns at their own speed.

It's easy to handle individual pace with individual teaching on the job. The new worker can work independently on a project until it is completed.

In the classroom, individual pace is more difficult to handle. You have to be the judge of how to pace your instruction. The faster students will get bored if you move too slowly. The slower ones will be discouraged if you move too fast.

How can you choose your pace? First of all, as you teach, watch your class for signs of impatience or confusion. Speed up or slow down as appropriate.

However, a major problem is that a pace that is too fast for some is too slow for others. One solution is to have extra work ready for those who complete their class work ahead of the others. They can work on more advanced problems, help slower classmates, or make teaching aids for future classes. Make sure the faster students don't view these extra assignments as penalties. Instead, present these special projects as a positive recognition of their speed and capability.

CONDITIONS YOU CREATE IN CLASS

The conditions just discussed are those you have to plan for ahead of time. But there are others you control during each session:

- Active learning

- Practice

- Frequent successes

- Correcting mistakes

- Self-esteem

- Competition

- Relating skills

- Understanding basics

Active Learning

Next to motivation, **active learning** is probably the most important condition for learning. Active learning means participation and hands-on work. Active learning is the opposite of passive learning.

Passive learning is simply receiving information. Passive learning includes things like listening to a lecture or watching a video.

In active learning, a student is actively doing things—trying new skills, working problems, or applying ideas.

Trainees who are insulating a pipe or laying out a sheet metal pattern are actively learning a new skill. They are also actively learning when they work math problems, give their opinion in a class discussion, or answer questions.

Practice

Practice is essential to learning. Probably at some time you have listened to an explanation of how to do something, sure that you understood it. Then when you tried to do it yourself, you became confused and frustrated. Just because you understand something (or think you do) doesn't mean you can do it. Practice is the only way we master a skill—whether it is a hand skill or a mental skill.

Practice isn't doing something once. Practice is doing a thing over and over again until the skill is mastered.

You have to give your trainees a chance to use important skills over and over again until they own them. It is not enough to give them the equation for calculating cubic feet and have them practice a few problems in class. They need practice and repeated practice until they can work problems with no difficulty. Give them homework assignments; give them problems to work at the start or end of another class; require them to figure cubic feet on jobs in the shop.

When they learn new hand skills for a project, have them repeat a project or do a similar one until they can perform at an acceptable level.

Frequent Successes

A good teacher sets up conditions that guarantee **frequent** and **early** successes. A student who feels successful one time is set up for success the next time and the next and the next. Each success builds up enthusiasm and confidence. A successful student is motivated for continued success.

On the other hand, a discouraged student is likely to become a major liability—one with a bad attitude who disrupts class and makes teaching miserable for you. Every failure affects motivation—especially if the failure is due to being overwhelmed with too much to learn. Occasionally a well-deserved failure can shock someone into making more effort. More often a failure is simply discouraging.

How do you create successes? First of all, plan short steps of learning. Make sure you feed the class small bites of learning that they can chew, swallow, and digest. Give them a chance to spend time on each new piece of learning. If it is information they get in the classroom, they need time to talk about it and examine all aspects of it. If it is a hand skill, they need time to practice it until it comes easy.

Second, they need to know that they have mastered the material. In the classroom, give them a chance to demonstrate that they know what you taught. Have them explain a process to the class or sketch a procedure on the board. Have them take a quiz that covers the lesson. In the lab, give them a chance to complete a project that demonstrates their skills. Make sure you acknowledge new accomplishments and encourage those who are struggling to succeed.

If your teaching goes well, most of them will have enough success to keep their enthusiasm and confidence growing. If too many don't do well, you'd better question what went wrong.

Correcting Mistakes

Students actively involved in learning will make mistakes. That's to be expected. Mistakes should be corrected immediately. A student who learns to do something the wrong way will require a lot of unlearning before starting over again to learn it the right way.

As your students practice—either in the shop or in the classroom—you must constantly check their work in order to correct mistakes. Do this with tact! Be careful not to embarrass them. Your primary goal is simply to give them the correct information or skills. Reassure them that making mistakes is a normal part of learning.

If your students expect to be ridiculed or embarrassed any time they make a mistake, they will be reluctant to say or try anything. Then all your efforts to promote active learning are bound to fail as well.

On the other hand, if your students are confident that their mistakes will be corrected in a helpful, professional manner, they will be eager to jump into any activity. It's up to you to set the tone so that they all feel comfortable learning—making mistakes and having those mistakes corrected.

It's not difficult to watch progress in the shop or lab and correct mistakes as soon as they occur. But you do have to circulate and stay alert to catch problems early on.

Keeping track of progress in a classroom is a different matter. One way to do it is to encourage participation and discussion in class. Another way is to give a quiz at the end of each session to see if they truly understand what you covered. Make sure that they see this simply as a way to check progress, not a challenge or a threat. A quiz should be simple to take and easy to correct. You can even have the students correct their own papers as you read the answers. Or you can have them exchange papers and correct each other's papers.

If you collect the quizzes, use them to see how each student is doing. But you should also use them to see how well your teaching is doing. If the whole class does poorly on a quiz, it may be that you didn't teach what you wanted to teach. Check your teaching and correct your own mistakes.

Self-Esteem

Someone with a good sense of self-esteem will have the motivation to do well in class. You can help your students to build a stronger sense of self-esteem.

Anyone who has a string of failures can easily develop a losing attitude and stop trying, thinking "I can't do this stuff—I'm too dumb." Part of your job is to make each one feel successful and worthwhile.

One of the best things you can do for the class as a whole is to remind them that you too were a beginner once. Tell them about particular problems you had. Give them confidence that they can master the skills and knowledge they are studying.

Even more important, you need to give everyone the boost of an individual compliment once in a while. Almost everyone does at least one thing well. Spotlight the successes. Display completed projects that are well done. Have a student demonstrate a skill for the rest of the class. Give compliments for a good answer in class or for good work on a project.

Spread your comments around. It's easy to praise your best students. You have to try a little harder to encourage your slower ones. But they are the ones who need encouragement the most. Tell them when their work is improving, and try to find those skills they do best.

Be even-handed in your praise. Some of your trainees will be a trial and a torment to you. You'll find it hard to say anything good about their work. But it may be that if you have a good word for them occasionally, their efforts and abilities will improve.

Competition

Competition can promote learning. But it can also kill it by discouraging those who are consistently on the bottom. You have to control competition in your class.

Having the worst student compete with the best is a sure way to completely discourage the weaker one. Grades are often a source of bad competition because they make grades rather than learning the important goal. Grading can be an incentive for some, but a road block for others.

Encourage your students to strive for their own personal best. Have them try to increase their speed on a particular job or their score on a test. Set them up to compete with themselves instead of one another.

Relating Skills

Relating new skills to old ones is a good way to get the knowledge to sink in. If you can show your students that a new skill is very similar to a skill they've already mastered, they will learn much more quickly.

Connections may be obvious to you, but they may not be obvious to your students. To them everything is new. So point out the similarities. This will make the amount they have to learn seem less overwhelming, and it will save teaching time for you.

Understanding Basics

Make sure that your students understand the basic concepts behind the facts and skills they are learning. If they understand the general principles, they are more likely to remember the particular facts. If they understand **why** something is done, they are likely to remember **how** it is done.

For example, if they understand the concept that wet materials contract as they dry out, they will understand why plaster or concrete may crack if it dries out too fast. They will be able to relate this idea to all kinds of plasters and cements that they use.

SUMMARY

You have to control the conditions that can make your class a success.

Some conditions—motivation, ability, and attitude—your students bring with them. You may not be able to change these completely. But you can find ways to motivate them, and if you get to know your students, you can get each one of them to do as much as they are able to do.

Some conditions you set up before class. That means planning and preparation. It's time well spent. Your class will run efficiently, and your students will really master what you teach.

Some conditions you create during class. These are the skills you use to get the class involved in learning, motivated to do the best job they can, and learning to the full extent of their ability.

No easy formula guarantees complete success. Teaching is still an art, and it's not always easy to do what needs to be done.

But if you really pay attention to your teaching, if you really try to set up the best possible conditions for learning, your classes will work. The people you train will be a credit to your teaching. It could be the most important and satisfying job you ever do.

Chapter 2

DO THE FOUR-STEP

THE FOUR STEPS OF INSTRUCTION

If you have already taught, you may have heard of the Four Steps of Instruction. If you have, don't stop reading just yet. I hope to give you a new way of looking at the Four Steps that will make your teaching more interesting and more effective.

If you haven't heard of the Four Steps, you should. They will improve your teaching and give you a well-organized approach to every lesson you teach.

You will probably see different versions of these steps, but they vary only in terminology. All of them follow the same general steps:

- **INTRODUCTION**—Create an interest and a need for learning.

- **PRESENTATION**—Present the new knowledge or skills.

- **APPLICATION**—Have students practice using the new material.

- **TEST**—Check to see what has been learned.

The Four Steps of Instruction have been around for a long time—at least fifty years. The Four Steps are a standard formula for teaching any subject. The Steps work—and work well—for both new and experienced teachers.

But any teaching formula dies if you always teach a class in the same way. New teachers may try to follow the Four Steps too routinely. After they become experienced, the Steps seem to limit what they would like to do, so they may decide that creative teaching doesn't follow the Four Steps. They dismiss them as something only for beginners.

The truth is that all good teaching follows the Four Steps—but experienced teachers blend and mix them so that they are not readily recognized. The steps are based on a recognition of why students learn. If you use the Four Steps, you create most of the conditions that help your class learn.

THE INTRODUCTION

A good introduction will arouse interest in the subject—it will make the student **want** to learn. You can do this in many ways: challenging the learner, arousing curiosity, raising questions that seem unanswerable, and many other techniques. The purpose of the introduction is not to teach new material, but to set the stage for it.

Standing in front of the class and saying, "This is important—you really need to learn this," is NOT an introduction. That's just another ho-hum phrase they've heard too many times before. The introduction has to get their attention and their interest. It hooks them—it makes them want to know more.

The old story of the farmer breaking a 2 x 4 over the mule's head "just to get his attention" is appropriate. You must do more than tell your class, "This is important." Shock them; startle them; get them upset; challenge them; give them problems they can't solve without more learning; ask questions they can't answer;

pose problems they can see are practical; have them try a new skill.

If you skip the introduction, you drastically cut down your opportunity to teach. A lot less learning takes place if the class studies a lesson just because you tell them to do it. Most of them will cooperate and go through the motions of learning because you expect them to. But your teaching is much more effective when they are interested and excited about learning a new subject that they **know** they need.

Here are a few ways to awake interest and a real desire to learn something new:

- Show how it applies to the job. Tell stories of how you used it on the job to save time and trouble. Tell stories of how **not knowing** cost a lot of extra time and problems on the job.

- Demonstrate interesting and useful things that can be done with the new knowledge or skill.

- Show that it will be needed for future projects.

- Share your enthusiasm.

- Ask questions designed to show the class that they really do need to know this new knowledge or skill.

The introduction builds **motivation**. Take a look at how television commercials build interest and motivation. Suddenly you want to try a product that a few moments ago you never heard of—because the car, perfume, or shampoo is going to make you a more exciting, desirable person; or it is going to give you something to your advantage. Add honesty to the television technique and you have a perfect introduction.

THE PRESENTATION

Your goal is to present new material in the most effective way.

This means using all the good teaching techniques available. You'll learn lots of them later on in Chapters 3, 4, and 5.

The most important thing to remember is that learning should be an **active** process. If you are the only one doing any work during class, there won't be much learning going on.

Teaching is more than telling. Don't just stand in front of the class and tell them what you want them to know. This is probably the most common teaching error. Students aren't empty buckets you can pour knowledge into. This does not mean that talking is not an important part of teaching. But if they just sit passively while you do all the talking, you will never hold their attention or their interest.

Your trainees have to **participate** in the learning process. This doesn't mean that they learn only when they are involved in a physical activity such as cutting a rafter or placing concrete for a foundation or programming a computer. They certainly learn then, but they are also actively involved when sitting in a classroom if they are answering questions, arguing a point in the lesson, or solving a problem.

Other media (what used to be called audiovisual aids) can be an important part of the presentation. But make the class active participants. Unless used carefully, such things as videos or DVDs can put your students to sleep or passively amuse them. Overhead transparencies or computer presentations are preferable—used correctly, they make it easy for you to get everyone actively involved.

APPLICATION

Application gives your students a chance to try out what they have learned. **Practice** in using new knowledge or skills is one of the most effective means of learning. When students actually try out a new procedure, they really make that knowledge their own.

This step can take many forms. You can have a student perform a task such as setting up a computer spread sheet or laying out a sheet metal pattern. You could give them practical, on-the-job math problems. Or you might simply ask them to tell you how they could manage a particular situation.

Sometimes the application will show that your students haven't learned all you expected them to know. Usually, all you have to do is to repeat a small part of the lesson so that they understand, or you may have to show some of them what they are doing wrong. However, if the whole class has misunderstood a major part of your presentation, you probably have to do a major part of the teaching over again.

Remember that application is NOT testing—it is part of the learning process. People often genuinely feel that they understand all the material until they have a chance to actually apply it. Then they find that they misunderstood, or they see a problem that they did not anticipate and they become confused. Give them a chance to practice their new knowledge and to correct their mistakes before you test them.

TEST

Testing helps your students see how much they have actually learned. Even more important, it lets you see how well you have taught.

Testing is often similar to application. The difference is that in testing, the student is expected to perform without help. During application, you are ready to correct errors and to help.

Don't think of testing as only the usual written test. A test can be making something or performing a task, such as setting up a job on a lathe. You can give an oral test by asking questions about the lesson, or by hearing their reactions in a class discussion. Transparencies can be used to give an identification test: make transparencies of objects or tools for the class to identify.

Use each test to improve your teaching. Testing can show you where your students need more help. You may discover that your teaching is going too fast for the entire class.

Use each test to review individual progress. If one student always does poorly on written tests but does very well at answering questions in class, you might suspect a reading problem. In that case, try different testing arrangements for that student. If another who has been doing well suddenly starts failing, you might look for an emotional problem, family problem, job problem, or some other outside cause for the sudden slump.

Don't fall into the trap of assuming that the students are stupid or not trying when all their test scores are low. Remember the saying, "If the learners haven't learned, the teacher hasn't taught." Like most sayings, it is not completely true, but there certainly is a lot of truth in it. Check your teaching and check your tests. Check for questions that haven't been thoroughly covered in class, or ones that aren't worded clearly. If they don't understand what you're asking, they can't possibly give you the right answer.

Some students may not learn because of serious emotional problems. Some may not have the necessary background to learn the material. (You can't teach percentages to someone who doesn't know how to multiply.) But if most of the class fails a test, it is usually an indication that there is something wrong with your teaching.

It's a shock to give the class a quiz and learn that all your great teaching has passed completely over their heads. You sit and wonder where the class was when you gave that brilliant, carefully prepared lecture. This happens to most teachers a time or two. When it happens, don't give in to all the miserable thoughts of quitting teaching, flunking the whole class, or telling them how stupid they are. Look at it as part of the learning experience. Without the test, you would still assume that they had learned the material. The test shows you the problem, and it gives you a chance to solve it.

USING THE FOUR STEPS

Remember that when you use the Four Steps, it's not a simple formula for paint-by-numbers teaching. In fact, if you stick to a rigid sequence, you and your class will find the Four Steps a bore. The illustration on this page shows some of the ways that the Four Steps can be combined in different sequences.

There should always be an introduction at (or nearly at) the start of a lesson. If you want to teach them you have to make them **want** to learn.

The most effective introduction is one that is not obviously an introduction. Some of the best use another one of the Four Steps as the introduction. Think of a movie you have seen that did not start with the usual titles and credits. Instead it started with a few minutes of the start of the action of the film. Then when you were hooked, the titles and credits came on and finally the movie started. You can use the procedure for Presentation, Application, and Test Steps in the same way.

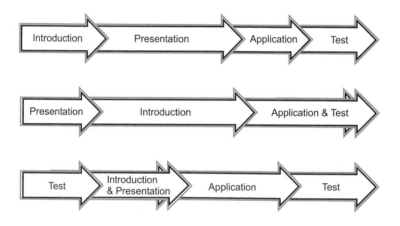

For example, suppose you were going to teach how to use a soldering gun. You could use any of the following steps as an INTRODUCTION:

- **Presentation**: Demonstrate how easy it is to use a soldering gun.

- **Application**: Without instruction, have a beginner try to use a soldering gun.

- **Test**: Ask a student to explain in detail how to use a soldering gun.

You could use any of the steps as an INTRODUCTION for a lesson on hand tools:

- **Presentation**: Show a transparency of several different hand tools and tell them that they must know the names and uses of all these.

- **Application**: Hold up one of the more uncommon hand tools and ask someone to describe its use.

- **Test**: Show a transparency of hand tools without any identifying names. Ask a student to name a tool and give its use.

Get their attention. Get them interested. Get them motivated. However you do it, your introduction needs to get them ready to learn, to work, and to pay attention.

In the same way, the presentation can also be combined with the other steps. In fact, all of the Four Steps can be rolled up into one operation.

For example, for the lesson on the soldering gun, the entire lesson may consist of showing how a soldering gun is used, then handing out a soldering gun and saying, "Practice using this on scrap metal. When you are comfortable with it, solder these fittings." The INTRODUCTION is brief because the students are already motivated since they know this is a useful job skill. The

PRESENTATION is mixed up with the APPLICATION. The worker tries to apply the skill, while you correct the efforts and demonstrate the proper way to do it. The TEST occurs when you see the worker finally demonstrate mastery of the skill.

The Four Steps may be stretched over several class sessions. For example, at the end of one lesson you may give the INTRODUCTION to the next lesson because the class will be reading the new lesson as homework and you want to be sure they see a need for doing it. The next class session may be spent entirely on the PRESENTATION, with the APPLICATION and TEST given the next day. In some cases the TEST might be delayed and given after two or more lessons are completed.

Just as the total length of time for any one lesson can vary, the relative length of the different steps can vary.

For example, for a hands-on project, your trainees may already know that the new skill is useful and interesting, so the introduction can be short. The presentation and the application of the new skill will be combined.

A HANDS-ON PROJECT

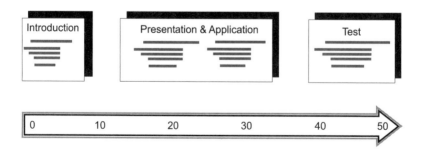

On the other hand, for a session on math, you might have to work harder to convince your students that this will be useful and interesting. You might need a longer, livelier introduction. The presentation may be fairly short, but there should be plenty of time for the application because they need plenty of practice. Make sure you plan enough time for testing.

A MATH LESSON

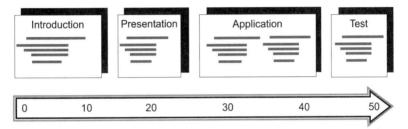

SUMMARY

The Four Steps of Instruction are essential because they create the basic conditions for learning:

- Motivation and interest

- Presentation of new facts or skills

- A chance to practice the new knowledge and correct errors

- A check on what has been learned

To be effective, you don't have to follow the steps by the numbers. They should be combined and varied according to your teaching situation.

CHECKLIST

- Take a fresh look at your students' hands-on projects. Look for ways to use all four steps for each project. Remember, depending on the situation, some steps can be shortened, lengthened, or combined.

- Look at lessons the class struggles with. Do you need to add to or change some of the Four Steps?

- Look for new ways to test your class—not to grade them, but to check on your teaching and find ways to improve it.

Plan new introductions for your lessons. Trial and error will show you which approaches work best with each class.

Chapter 3

GUIDE—DON'T PUSH

THE LEARNING MANAGER

Look back at your grade school experience. Most likely the teacher was a dictator (only a few steps below God) who controlled the classroom absolutely and who was the recognized authority on every subject. The teacher was the all-around expert who poured out knowledge while the students quietly soaked it up. That old-style teacher taught according to this old verse:

> Pour it in, pound it in,
> The students' heads are hollow.
> Pour it in, pound it in,
> There's much, much more to follow.

Today—probably because of the vastly greater body of knowledge that must be taught—the teacher is no longer expected to be an expert in every subject. Instead, teachers are trained to be **learning managers**. This means that the teacher, although still knowledgeable about the general subject, does not have to be an expert in every phase of it. The teacher still has to know the subject, but also has to know how to create learning conditions—both physical and psychological.

MANAGING YOUR CLASS

To be an effective learning manager, you must make sure that your students take an active part in the learning process. Students are not sponges that simply soak up all the knowledge you pour out.

A student is more like a computer: You feed in the knowledge and the computer digests it, applies it to problems, and turns it into solutions which it spits out. Your role is to feed in the information and punch the proper buttons to start the problem-solving process. You **guide** the process, but you don't do it all yourself.

You manage learning in your class in various ways. First of all, you have to manage the class and set up rules and conditions so that nothing interferes with the learning process. Second, you have to manage individual people—your students. You have to get to know them and steer them on the right course so that they are ready and able to use the knowledge you have to give them. Finally, you have to set up and manage your information, materials, and teaching techniques. They all have to fit your class and fit your goals.

As a learning manager you have to plan your class so that you can create and maintain the conditions for learning that were covered in Chapter 1. Your planning has to include everything from the course outline to classroom rules.

The Course Outline

The first step in planning is to set up a **course outline**. The course outline lists the subjects to be taught in the order they should be taught. Remember that learning should progress in short steps of instruction. The sequence of lessons should be designed to insure that students repeat skills and review knowledge learned in earlier lessons. Practice and review reinforces learning.

Write out your course outline with a calendar of your class schedule. Make sure you plan a time for everything on your course outline so that there are no important omissions and no duplications.

Class Rules

It's easy to overlook the mechanics of how you run your class, assuming that you'll do whatever feels right at the time. But if you don't decide ahead of time how you will operate the class, you may find that the class time gets frittered away without accomplishing as much as you planned. Good rules, based on common sense, are time savers.

Trivial routines such as calling roll, getting the class started, and giving coffee breaks can waste a lot of time that should be spent on instruction.

One of the biggest time wasters is often the process of getting the class cranked up and moving. Some classes go through a long slow process: the students dribble in gradually, talking and joking, while the instructor fumbles with notes and materials or joins in the joking. Plan a starting time that makes it possible for your class to arrive on time. Make sure **you** always arrive on time. If you're not on time, you can't expect your class to be on time. If you usually come five minutes late, your students will take to drifting in five to fifteen minutes late. However, if you arrive 10 to 15 minutes early, they'll see that you are serious about the class, and they will take it more seriously too.

This doesn't mean that you have to be grim and no-nonsense with your class all the time. Just don't let the class time be time for idle talk and time-wasting.

Keeping attendance records can be important, but calling roll at each class meeting holds up the entire class. Plan a more efficient way to check attendance, such as having a sign-in sheet, or giving a student the job of checking attendance. (Rotate the duty.)

A coffee break can eat up a big chunk of your teaching time unless you plan for it and manage it carefully. Even with the best of intentions, the break will begin to stretch from ten minutes to fifteen to twenty. In no time at all, it will be eating up half an hour of learning time. Decide how much time you want to allow for a coffee break and then **stick to it**. If you set a ten-minute break, let the class know that you will close the door and start teaching again after ten minutes of break—and do it!

The general rule to follow is to make no rules you cannot enforce or do not care to enforce. And don't set up rules that are almost impossible for the class to adhere to.

MANAGING PEOPLE

As a learning manager, you manage people. This means you need to know your students so you can help each one to learn as much as possible.

In a class of fifteen students, you are faced with fifteen different people with fifteen different reactions to everything you do. You can't stand in front of a group, deliver a lecture, and expect that all fifteen will understand what you are saying—or even want to. Some of them will be so eager and ready to learn that they will learn in spite of what you do. Others will be completely bored. And some may even be antagonistic.

How you handle each one is a matter of instinct, educated guess, and trial and error. For a few in your class, your job will be to assign a project and then stand back so that you don't get run over. Others must be guided each step of the way. Still others must be driven by threats.

Checklist:

- Get to know each student as an individual so you can choose the best approach for teaching.

- Not everyone can learn the same amount. If you know your students, you can judge when one has reached peak performance and when another is just coasting.

- Problem students usually act up for a reason. If you can find out what the reason is, sometimes the problem can be solved by you or by someone you can refer the student to.

- Whether or not you find the reason behind problem behavior, sometimes you have to face the fact that one problem student is taking up too much time from the rest of the class. You may have to remove the problem from your class.

- Set goals that are just beyond the reach of each individual. These will be of different degrees of difficulty. Don't make it too easy for the best students or too hard for the poorer ones.

- Be flexible. Don't let your first impression of a student color everything you see. Your first impression may well change over time, and you must be prepared to set new goals or take a different approach.

- Your job is to make everyone **want to learn**.

Managing People Problems

If you are well-organized and using good teaching techniques you will probably maintain control of your class without much difficulty. However, there comes a time in every teacher's life when there is a "problem child" in the class. The "problem child" may be fifty years old and the problem may range from talking in class to challenging everything you say. When it comes, don't look at it as a threat to your authority but rather as an unfair infringement on the rights of other students to learn.

There is no way to give specific directions on handling every kind of problem you may run into. On any classroom problem, it is easy to let anger take over and get into a nose-to-nose shouting match with the troublemaker. This only disrupts the class and builds even more antagonism. There are some good, solid rules to follow that will avoid problems, solve, or diffuse them.

The most effective procedure is to avoid problems before they start:

- Make sure your class rules are clear and discuss them with the students.

- Do not make more rules than absolutely necessary. Each one creates problems of enforcement, and each one creates problems of judgment about extenuating circumstances.

- Every rule must be enforced.

- Do not make rules or threats that you cannot—or are unwilling to—back up.

- Think out the consequences of each rule.

- Catch potential problems as early as possible and discuss them with those concerned.

Solving Problems

You can't solve a problem until you know what the problem is. You may think that your problem is a loud-mouth troublemaker who just likes to keep things stirred up. In reality, you may have a student who can't read and is trying to hide the problem with loud or disruptive behavior.

Avoid public confrontations whenever possible. You may have to tell a student that their behavior is interfering with the rest of the class and that it must stop. But you are not going to solve the problem with a public confrontation. You might put a lid on it temporarily, but you won't solve a thing.

Whenever you have problems in class, try to solve them in private on a one-to-one basis. When you have a conference with a problem student, the first priority is to find out what the problem really is. Usually it is something outside of class—such as financial trouble, personal problems, or illiteracy. Even if you can't solve the problem, you can help by being a good listener. That alone can be the start of a solution.

MANAGING LEARNING

As a learning manager, you have to create the best possible conditions for learning. You don't simply hand out pre-packaged bits of information. Instead, you set up opportunities to get your students involved so that they have a chance to learn.

Hands-on projects in the shop or lab guarantee active learning. Make sure you set up a good sequence of learning with small steps of instruction and enough time for practice. Your students should have a clear objective, such as applying a plaster coat, adjusting a carburetor, testing an electronic circuit, or setting up a computer mailing list. You manage the mechanics of the project by making all the supplies and equipment available. In short, you create the ideal conditions for successful learning. At this point you can step back and let the students learn. But while they work, circulate, correct mistakes, offer suggestions, praise improvements, and above all, encourage their enthusiasm.

In the classroom, it's not as easy to get them involved. Your challenge is to reduce the amount of lecture time and to devise ways to make them active—not just passive—learners. Some subjects, such as math, naturally lend themselves to student involvement because once an equation is explained and demonstrated, the natural step is to have them work problems. However, you can go a step beyond this.

Consider two approaches to the same lesson. Suppose your goal is to teach your class how to calculate the area of a circle using the equation $A = \pi \times R^2$. This is an easy goal because it naturally gets the students actively involved in applying the knowledge by calculating the area of circles.

The old way to teach this lesson would be to write the equation on the board, work some sample problems, have the class work some problems, and give a test.

The better way to teach the lesson would also include an explanation of how or when the equation is used. It could include some (but probably not all) of the following activities:

- Have them discuss whether π should be used as 3.14, 3.1416, or $3\frac{1}{7}$, based on the degree of accuracy they need.

- Have them check to see if there are other ways to calculate or estimate the area of a circle—ways that are as good or better for some circumstances. (There are.)

- Have teams work problems, check answers with each other, and determine the reasons for errors.

- Have teams or individuals write practical problems that use the equation.

- Have teams measure circular objects around the building and calculate their area.

It's true that both methods will teach the students the equation, because both get them using the knowledge. But with the second method, they are more actively involved in the learning process. They will have a better grasp of the subject and are likely to remember the material longer.

Managing Guest Teachers

What about class subjects where you're not an expert? In this rapidly changing world, this will happen more and more. No one can be expert in all the many and new technologies in the craft. You may have to teach a subject you really don't know much about.

No problem. You are a learning manager—not a universal expert. You know how to set up conditions that allow students to learn. There are several ways to teach an unfamiliar subject:

- Assigning readings and reports

- Gathering manufacturers' literature to analyze and discuss

- Assigning students to interview knowledgeable persons

- Inviting other knowledgeable persons to sit in on the class to answer questions

Another way to manage an unfamiliar subject is to bring in an expert. Some of your colleagues, or employees, or even one of your students may well be skilled in the subject. Manufacturers and salesmen can also be a good source of expertise.

Just remember that guest teachers can be a disaster. They can talk too long. They are usually disorganized. They generally tell instead of teach. But you are the manager. You are responsible for maintaining learning conditions in your class. You need to plan carefully, and diplomatically, to make sure that your guest will work within the framework that you control:

- Set the objectives and review them with the guest teacher.

- Discuss the procedure with the guest and talk about ways in which to involve the class. Remember that the guest will probably be an amateur teacher who thinks that teaching is simply telling.

- Have the guest give you an outline of what will be covered. If possible, sit down with the guest teacher ahead of time and work out an outline together.

- Set the time for the guest to use and be prepared to enforce the time schedule.

- Be prepared to ask the class controversial questions about the subject that will spark a discussion.

- At the end of the guest teacher's presentation, summarize the subject and ask the class some questions about it.

SUMMARY

You are not a walking data bank—you are a **learning manager**:

- You plan your course so that you have an effective outline of subjects to teach, and you plan rules that make your class time effective learning time.

- You manage your students, treating them as individuals with individual problems and abilities, so that you can suit your teaching to their needs.

- You manage the class and lab to make the best learning conditions possible.

Chapter 4

TRICKS OF THE TRADE

PRESENTATION SKILLS AND TEACHING TECHNIQUES

What do you do once you are in front of your class? In this chapter I'll tell you some of the tricks of the trade that I have learned. These principles will make you more confident and effective whenever you are making a presentation in front of a group. How you present yourself and how you present your material affect how well your students learn.

PRESENTATION SKILLS

Teaching is communicating—transferring our knowledge and skills to others. Our communication skills determine how effective we are in all of the Four Steps of Instruction. In conducting teacher training classes, I have found that a few lucky persons are just naturally masters at communication. However, most (like me) have to work hard at becoming effective communicators. Even if you rate yourself very high in communication skills, you can probably increase your effectiveness in the classroom.

Find Your Place

Your location in the classroom has a lot to do with your

relationship with the class. It determines whether you are seen as an authority separate from the students, or seen as a member of the group, participating in a learning process.

If you remain behind a table or podium, you separate yourself from the class. This is not necessarily bad—just be aware of what it says to the class. It's fine for such things as a formal lecture, or a presentation of a scientific or technical paper.

Moving away from the protection of the podium or table will get you closer to the students. And it tends to give you confidence because you start to feel part of the group. Walking around the room among the students and even sitting with them brings the students closer to you. And there is a bonus—it gives you confidence because you start to feel you are talking with friends.

Appearance and Body Language

Your appearance is the first thing your class notices about you. That's why you should dress neatly and appropriately. If you are addressing a group of professional people, a suit probably fits the occasion. If your class is a group of service technicians who are coming directly from the job, your clothes should be more informal. The point is that your appearance lets the group relate to you. Your clothes should not set you apart from the group.

Almost all of us are nervous in front of a new group. The trick is not to show it. After the first few minutes, most of us get over the nerves. An effective cure for the nerves is to pick one person in the class and talk directly to that person until you complete a thought. Then shift to another person and do the same thing. In this way you are having a conversation with one person instead of that scary entire class. Being confident that you know your material also helps control nervousness. If you work at appearing calm and relaxed, at some point in your presentation you will suddenly realize that you actually are—and enjoying the experience.

Be aware of your body language. All of us have bad habits that we are unaware of and that can communicate the wrong message. Hands on hips can convey nervousness or hostility.

Your arms crossed in front of you also says you are nervous and feel defensive.

For most of us, hands become a big problem in front of a class. Whatever we do with them seems awkward and artificial. Experts say that when you are standing, your hands should be relaxed and by your side. I'm not sure this is always true. My advice is to watch the pros on television and see what they do. They use various positions such as hands clasped in front of them, or one hand by the side and the other half raised. Learn what is natural for you and practice doing that when you speak. If you are sitting at a table, your hands should be relaxed and resting on the table. Guard against fiddling with pencils, pointers and other such things.

The very best way to improve your communication ability is to set up a video camera to record yourself while you are teaching a lesson. Then view it by yourself. This will let you see yourself as the students see you. You will probably be surprised at all the dumb things you are doing without realizing it—I know I was. I do this in my teacher training classes. I remember one student who was absolutely amazed to see that he was wringing his hands continuously through his entire lesson.

Delivery

When you record your presentation, pay attention to the audio. It will give you insight on ways to improve your speech delivery. Look for things like these:

- Verbal tics (um, you know, okay?)
- Your rate of speech (Nervous people talk too fast.)
- Variation in tone and sound level. A monotone is deadly.
- Clear speech. Are you pronouncing words clearly?
- Voice pitch. A low mumble or a shrill voice will turn your students off.

Eye contact is extremely important. Don't look at the ceiling or gaze off into space. And don't do the opposite—talk continuously to one person. Look at and talk to an individual while you complete one thought or answer a question. Then move on to another person. Ideally, you should talk to each individual in the class. When you find that you are talking to different individuals and feeling relaxed, you've got it made.

Above all, keep your sense of humor and respect your students. Be able to laugh at yourself when you goof. Enjoy a joke with the class. But don't tell jokes just for the sake of a joke. Use them only if they illustrate a point—and keep them short. Remember your goal is to teach—not just to entertain. I have had teachers who were natural storytellers and comedians and they kept their class in stitches. The students really enjoyed themselves—until at the end of the class they suddenly realized that they had not learned anything.

But always laugh WITH the students—not AT them. Respect the dignity of each student. Don't argue, deride, or humiliate. When a student speaks, even it is a wrong answer or an outlandish opinion, use some of a teacher's stock phrases like these:

- Thank you.
- That's an interesting viewpoint.
- How many agree with that?
- How did you arrive at that?
- Explain more about that.

Another way is to ask questions—to have the student clarify the statement; to learn how the opinion was arrived at; or to guide the student into finding the right answer.

Your choice of language can offend and therefore turn students off. Never use profanity. And avoid religious and political comments. Use conversational language—don't try to impress. If you use new terms, acronyms, or trade jargon, write the terms on the board and explain them. Avoid tentative words that convey indecision (maybe, hopefully, perhaps, probably).

Finally, here are some rules and reminders:

- Smile. Enjoy yourself. Even if you don't feel that way, fake it and soon you will feel it happen.

- Use gestures sparingly and only use those that are natural to you. Watch that you do not repeat the same gesture continuously.

- In most situations, it's best to move around the room.

- Talk to individuals, not to space.

- Use a conversational tone. Students should feel that you are talking directly to them.

- Occasionally you will get a question that you cannot answer. Don't try to fake it—students can see right through that. If it's a factual question and no one in the class knows the answer, I found its best to simply say, "I don't know, but I'll find out." If the question requires an opinion, refer it to the class for discussion.

- If you are teaching adults, often someone in the class is an expert on a specific part of the subject. Don't be afraid to use a student expert as a resource.

- Avoid reading material unless you occasionally need to read a short quote from a book or paper.

- Vary your voice tone, volume, and expression.

- Use common words. Unusual words that are not needed do not impress—they confuse.

- Always face the class when you are talking to them.

- Keep the objectives of your Lesson Plan in mind. Don't let the class stray too far from the subject matter.

- When you answer a question from a student, include the whole class in your answer, not just the one person.

- Let your enthusiasm for the subject you are teaching show.

TEACHING TECHNIQUES

If you watched twenty different teachers teach the same subject, you would probably see twenty different methods of teaching—or at least, that's how it would seem. Actually, all teachers draw from the same arsenal of basic teaching techniques, but the difference shows in the varied ways they use and combine those techniques.

Just as the Four Steps of Instruction should be varied to suit your needs, these teaching techniques can be combined to suit your needs and your teaching style. Each technique has its own particular advantages and disadvantages—sometimes they are obvious, but sometimes they are not. It all boils down to having the right tool for the job—and knowing how to use it.

You should be able to use any of these teaching techniques:

- Lecture
- Guest speakers
- Student presentations
- Discussion
- Questions
- Role playing

LECTURE

Every course in education methods will tell you that lecturing is the worst method of teaching. The professor who tells you this invariably does it during a lecture.

Probably the idea that lectures are the poorest form of teaching came from the formal, university-type lecture. The professor walks into a large lecture hall filled with three or four hundred students, talks at them for an hour, and then leaves. The students sit and "absorb" the material—or nap. There is no active learning, no questions, and no discussion.

However, a lecture doesn't have to be a long sterile talk. Instead it can be one part of a balanced, well-organized lesson, which also might include questions, problem solving, and hands-on practice. Your lecture can be revved up with stories, chalkboard diagrams, and demonstrations.

Advantages and Disadvantages

Like anything else in teaching, too much lecture is a bad idea. In the first place, the quality of the lecture depends upon the skill of the speaker. A dull speaker, however expert and knowledgeable, can quickly put a class to sleep. On the other hand, a charismatic speaker, or one who is a great storyteller, is tempted to talk off the top of the head instead of using a prepared lesson plan. Entertainment is no substitute for information.

Second, if you depend entirely upon lecturing, you will never get to know your students. They will sit back and expect you to perform. Active teaching is no substitute for active learning.

A third pitfall is the temptation to make the lecture a repeat of the reading assignment. That tells the class that they don't need to read the assignment—you will give them a report on it. Don't **ever** read the textbook out loud. It is boring and insulting—and it shows that you are too lazy to prepare for class.

Above all, the chief disadvantage of too much lecturing is that the students are passive. If they sit with brains in neutral while you crank out information, little real learning will take place. **Keep them actively involved**.

In spite of all these potential disadvantages, lecture is sometimes the most effective way of teaching a large group (as long as it still gets the students involved in some way). It is an excellent technique for quickly conveying facts, ideas, concepts, and attitudes. A good lecture will provide knowledge beyond what's in the textbook, and it will keep a class interested and motivated.

Prepare Your Lecture

The key to good lecturing is careful preparation. In the long run, students prefer a carefully prepared lecture with substance to an amusing talk that teaches little. If—like most of us—you are an average speaker, take comfort in the fact that the knowledge in your carefully prepared lectures will be remembered long after the funny stories have been forgotten.

Of course, if you are a skilled speaker and you prepare your lecture material carefully, you can entertain and educate at the same time. But in a class, entertainment is a tool of learning—not an end in itself. When you lecture, plan what you'll teach and teach what you planned.

Checklist

1. Change pace often. Talk for a while, then use a transparency, ask questions, start discussions on controversial issues, or give a demonstration—anything to get the class involved. The amount of straight talking time should never exceed 15 minutes. You can't perform at top quality more than that, and the brain can't absorb more than the seat of the pants can endure.

2. Stop to ask questions and start discussions in order to find out if your class is still with you. Watch for confused looks, inattention, or talking in class. If they aren't learning from your lecture, stop it, change it, or try something else.

3. Don't just repeat a reading assignment. Expand on it. Bring it to life:

    - Explain points you think are not covered adequately in the text.

    - Answer questions.

    - Tie in personal experiences that illustrate some points.

    - Use real-life examples to show how textbook information is actually used.

- Explain how certain ideas and laws were discovered.

- Explain a related subject not covered by the text.

4. Consider the time of day. In general, a morning class will be bright and alert. You may be able to lecture and still keep their attention. Afternoon and evening classes tend to be tired and listless, and they usually require extra effort on your part (when you are also tired).

Students in job-related classes can usually see a real connection between the class work and their work on the job. Even in evening classes, after a hard day's work, they pay attention to a good lecture, mixed with some class activity. On the other hand, a poorly prepared lecture will receive little mercy from any class—morning, noon, or night.

Taking Notes From Your Lecture

Most people aren't skilled at taking notes. It's hard to write and listen at the same time. It is also hard to identify what is most important while the lecture is going on. Some will take no notes. Others will try to write down everything you say and their notes are about as useless as none.

Don't make your lecture a guessing game. Let the class know what is important and what you expect. Write key facts, equations, or terms on the chalkboard; don't jot on the board whatever comes to your mind, because they will assume it is important. Give them clues like these:

"This is important. I will ask for it on the test."

"You must know this equation from memory."

"I don't expect you to know this equation—just how to look it up and use it."

"You won't be expected to know these equations or how to use them. I am just showing you how the results are arrived at and what their relationship is."

To help them take notes, hand out a typed outline with space for additional personal notes. This ensures some organization to their notes. Or you can write an outline on the board as you lecture or have the outline on a transparency. Copying the outline forces the students to write it down—which is a guarantee that the item is read at least once.

GUEST SPEAKERS

If you have a specialized topic to teach, you may want to invite a guest speaker to your class. Technicians, specialists, other teachers, manufacturers' representatives, Red Cross workers, and many others can be valuable sources of information.

A guest speaker can be a disaster or a great success. Just remember that you are the learning manager and you have to keep control of the class. Refer to Chapter 3, The Learning Manager, for suggestions on controlling the situation. The key is to review the presentation with the guest speaker **before** the class. A guest speaker is likely to lecture at least part of the time, so all of the warnings and suggestions on lectures apply.

Guest speakers have two main drawbacks: they may bore the class to death or thoroughly confuse it. It is your responsibility—as diplomatically as possible—to rescue bad situations and get the speaker back on track.

Many guest speakers have a particular fish to fry. They may want to sell a product or bad-mouth another group. Try to avoid this problem when you select the speaker. Your preliminary meeting should make it clear that a guest teacher must be impartial and unbiased.

Like all of us, guest speakers love the sound of their own voice. Even when it's tough to get them started, it can be tougher yet to get them to stop. Show mercy to your students—be prepared to shut down the session—diplomatically, of course.

STUDENT PRESENTATIONS

Student presentations are like guest lectures in one way. You can ask a student to report on new materials, demonstrate a new process, or relate an interesting experience. In adult classes, you often find a student who has more knowledge and experience than you in a particular area. Make use of it.

Student presentations can take a lot of time. Consider the time required to have 20 members of a class each give a 10 minute report. Allowing at least 20 minutes for each presentation (for discussion, questions, transition time, etc.) means about $6\frac{1}{2}$ hours of class time. And you will squirm in your seat during many presentations because you know you could have done it better and faster.

Many of the warnings that apply to guest speakers apply to student presentations. As learning manager, you have to keep control of what goes on in your class. If you use student presentations as a lazy way of getting out of teaching, the results are likely to be a disaster.

However, there is much learning potential in these presentations. The others always seem to pay more attention and learn a great deal—probably because they can imagine themselves up these. The student giving the presentation always learns much more than those who are listening.

Perhaps the most important reason for student presentations is that many of your students are going to be leaders in the industry ten or fifteen years from now. You can give them a start in getting the skills and confidence they need to stand up and talk in front of a group.

Use student presentations sparingly, but use them.

DISCUSSION

A good discussion will get the whole class completely involved in the learning process. Everyone thinks, everyone talks, and everyone learns.

In a discussion, you should say very little. Let the class carry the discussion, with comments from one person triggering comments and opinions from others. Your role is to keep the discussion from running too far off the subject, and to ask questions to involve those who are reluctant to speak up.

Use discussion to think through problems or work out opinions. It is not useful for strictly factual material. The question, "If your partner comes on the job drunk, what should you do?" is a good subject for discussion. On the other hand, "How do you sharpen a twist drill?" or "How do you set up a transit level?" are not good discussion subjects because they require a recital of facts, not opinions or attitudes.

Brainstorming is a form of discussion where anyone comes up with ideas on a given topic. These can be jotted down on the chalkboard or overhead, with no criticism or discussion until all possible ideas have been laid out. Then all items are discussed, compared, and evaluated.

Discussion can also be used as an INTRODUCTION step to get the class involved in a problem and aware that they need more information. It can also be used in the APPLICATION step to help the class formulate opinions or develop ways to solve a problem. It can even be used in the TEST step to determine what's been learned.

Advantages and Disadvantages

The advantage of discussion is that it can get the class totally involved in active learning. It makes them think, and it can help them form attitudes and opinions on difficult subjects.

Another advantage is that the discussion may go in directions and give results that you do not expect—or even do not want to hear. This can give you a new outlook on your teaching, let you understand your students better, and even change your own opinions.

One disadvantage is that sometimes a discussion just never gets off the ground. Some groups simply don't respond well to an open discussion. However, if you can get one or two students started, the rest will probably open up and join in.

On the other hand, some discussions get out of control and bog down in trivial comments and stories. As a learning manager you have to keep control of the situation and bring the class back on course.

Discussions can be full of surprises. Be prepared to accept the results even though they are not the ones you anticipated or hoped for. Common sense will tell you not to open up discussion on procedures that you will not or cannot change. Don't ask if the coffee break should be longer unless you are willing to abide by the group's decision!

Prepare for Discussion

Obviously, you can't just sit back and let the class go at it. A good discussion takes careful preparation and skill on your part.

Checklist

- Decide on the subject and purpose of the discussion.

- Write out a list of questions to start the discussion—or to restart it if it goes dead. They can't have yes or no answers or factual answers. Discussions will start when one person states an opinion and another disagrees with it. Avoid leading questions like, "Don't you think that . . . ." Instead say. "What do you think about . . . ."

- Don't give your opinion. Your job is to control and direct—not to take part. If you give your opinion, it will influence the group. Don't get drawn into arguments and don't take sides. If someone asks you a question, refer the question back to the group.

■ Keep the group directed to discussing and arguing ideas and opinions, and not to attacking a person.

■ For a large class, an alternate procedure is to divide it into small groups, then bring the groups together to report on the results of their discussions.

■ Watch for those who are not taking part and ask their opinion—especially on subjects in which they have experience. Assist someone who has a hard time expressing an idea by asking "Are you saying that . . . ?"

■ Don't let one or two people dominate the discussion.

■ Bring the group back to the subject if they stray too far. Sometimes you may let them stray if they get off on an important subject that relates to the general topic. At the end of the discussion, point out that they got off the subject but that it seemed an important direction.

■ Make a summary on the chalkboard of anything the group agrees on. Ask the group if this is what they can agree to.

QUESTIONING

Questions—and answers—are at the very heart of learning. Questions can and should be used in all four teaching steps. They can be used in the introduction to make the class realize that there is something important to learn. A well-framed question will lead your students in just the right directions.

Questioning can be used in the PRESENTATION step to check on understanding. It can be used in both the APPLICATION step ant TEST step to check on the class learning—and on your teaching. Also, proper questioning is the key to starting and continuing a good discussion. Like any other teaching technique, good questioning requires thought, practice, and preparation.

Plan questions carefully. Write them out and list them in a logical sequence. Have the list on hand during class, and add more questions during class as they occur.

Direct questions at specific people. Generally, the best method is to ask a question without calling on someone; pause to give the class time to think of the answer; then call on someone by name. This method makes all of them try to think of the answer because they might be called on. If you call on someone before you ask the question, the others won't bother to think about the answer.

Use **overhead questions** sparingly. An overhead question is directed at the whole class, asking for volunteers to answer. Overhead questions allow those with the greatest interest in the subject to answer, and they avoid embarrassing anyone. They are useful for difficult or controversial questions. The danger is that they let the more talkative (not necessarily the brightest) students dominate the class. Nevertheless, if combined with **direct questions** (calling upon a specific person to answer) overhead questions are valuable.

Don't use questions to ridicule your students. This makes learning a source of fear and embarrassment. Don't use questions to pounce on inattentive students, to embarrass those who you suspect have not done their assignment, or to embarrass someone who obviously doesn't understand the material. When the students don't know the answers, help them out of a difficult situation without destroying their dignity.

Use questions to encourage the shy students to participate. Be careful the questions don't discourage them instead. Ask questions at first that you are sure they can answer. If a student can't answer, ease out of the situation without adding further embarrassment. One method is to answer the question yourself. Another is to give clues to the answer through additional questions.

Avoid yes or no questions. Instead of asking, "Is this drawing right?", ask, "What would you add to this drawing?" Instead of asking, "Is this the best way to do this?" ask, "How would you do this?"

Don't ask, "Are there any questions?" The class rarely responds. No one wants to ask a dumb question. Usually, only a very aggressive student will respond to such an opening. Instead, be open to any questions that come up during your classes. Don't make anyone feel stupid for asking a question. That's a sure way to cut off all questions from the whole class.

Use questions about hands-on projects. They are a good device to throw the responsibility of evaluating a project back onto the student. Ask questions like these:

"What would you do differently the next time you do this?"

"How would you rate the quality of your work on this project?"

"Where do you think this needs improvement?"

Questions will also show if a student understands why the project was done in a certain way:

"Why does this method work?"

"Explain what you did and why you did it."

"Can you think of a better way to do this?"

"What would happen if this were left out?"

ROLE PLAYING

Role playing is a technique in which you set up an imaginary situation and assign students to play the roles of the people in the situation. For example, you might describe a situation in which a worker is always late for work. Then assign one student to play the worker and another student to play the foreman who has to deal with the problem. The two then act out the roles in class. Afterward, discuss the situation with the class.

Role playing should not be used frequently, and you may not feel comfortable using it at all. However, it is an effective way to teach human relations problems, such as how to deal with a worker who comes on the job drunk or on drugs.

Learning comes from several sources. The students playing the roles get experience in dealing with people to solve problems. The rest of the class learns by observation. Probably the greatest source of learning is the class discussion that follows the role playing. Ask the class how well the role players handled the situation and what might have been done differently.

Be careful who you pick for role-playing. A showboater may just want to show off or may not take the assignment seriously. A very shy or unwilling student may not be able to get into the role. If you know your students, you will know which to choose, and which ones to avoid.

INDIVIDUALIZED INSTRUCTION

Everyone learns at a different pace and in a different way. **Individualized instruction** allows students to learn in their own way and at their own pace. Every student is provided with a learning unit and allowed to learn the material independently at an appropriate rate.

Traditional group instruction gives students a set time to learn a set amount of material. Those who don't learn it all by the scheduled time get a lower grade and miss out on a lot of learning. With individualized instruction, each student can learn the lesson thoroughly because each student takes as much time as needed to learn it.

Instructors who teach apprentice classes or other shop courses use individualized instruction to some extent simply because of the nature of the class. Often apprentices in the same class are in different years of apprenticeship and therefore in different stages of learning. In addition, the shop work part of a course is all individual instruction simply because the students will need different lengths of time to complete each project. The result is that soon each one is working on a different project.

For individualized instruction, the instructor has to prepare a learning package to cover each lesson, using the Four Steps of Instruction. A student works on one learning package at a time, learning it thoroughly, and then proceeds to the next. This technique places the emphasis on learning instead of grading.

Advantages and Disadvantages

The main disadvantage of individualized instruction is that it requires a lot of preparation time for the teacher. A good textbook can help, but even then, the teacher must develop an assignment sheet that tells the students what to read and do, and a test to check learning. As soon as one learning package, or chapter, is complete, another one has to be ready to give out. The teacher has to keep track of which students have completed which lessons. This requires a well-maintained filing and record-keeping system.

As with any other technique, you can have too much of a good thing. If you make your entire course into individualized learning packages and do nothing but hand out papers and mark progress, the student might as well be taking a correspondence course.

However, when balanced with all the other teaching techniques, individualized instruction provides a good way to teach subjects that are necessary but difficult to teach. It places an emphasis on thorough learning instead of fast learning.

PROJECTS

In classes where most teaching takes place in the shop or lab, projects are often used.

However, projects must be selected carefully so that they enlist all the skills that the student must master. They must also require the student to repeat the most important operations so that they gain skills through repetition. Projects must be arranged in the proper sequence on the principle of short steps of instruction, so that each project builds upon the knowledge and skills gained from the previous ones.

Keep track of your students' progress on projects by making a progress chart. Chapter 5 gives you practical points for using a progress chart.

Some projects are so simple that verbal directions are best. "Sharpen this drill" or "Cut that pipe" may be all the instruction needed, since you will be there to instruct and correct. More complicated projects, such as troubleshooting an electronic circuit or setting up a computer spread sheet, may require detailed instructions and drawings of exactly what is to be done and how the finished project should look. These instructions are generally called **job sheets**. Page 63 has an example of a job sheet.

DEMONSTRATION

Demonstrations are a valuable and natural part of instruction. You are constantly demonstrating how to do things in the lab. On the job, a new hand learns by informal demonstration. Ideally, an experienced worker does a job and the new hand helps and watches how it is done—and then gets a chance to do it under supervision.

When you have a group who will all be doing the same operation (such as booting up a computer) you can save time by demonstrating certain key operations. When equipment or tools are too limited for everyone in class to do an operation, a demonstration is the next best thing.

Many of your demonstrations are spur-of-the-moment and one-on-one in the shop or lab. However, whenever you demonstrate something in the shop for a student, get more mileage out of it and call others who are in the same general stage of development to come watch.

A demonstration is really an active lecture. Ask questions as you go along. Let different students try a process while you help and correct. Or, have a student give a demonstration. The class will often pay closer attention to another student—perhaps because they want to see a fellow student succeed.

TESTING

Tests and quizzes can be used just for grading or they can go to work as a useful teaching technique. Tests help students to see what they really learned, and they help you to see how effective your teaching was.

It goes without saying that you must write reasonable test questions. They must relate clearly to what you've taught, and they must be easy to read and understand. The following sequence shows how a test can be used as a teaching tool. As you will see, the test itself is only the starting point.

1.   After a class presentation, give a short objective quiz.

2.   When they have finished it, tell the class that there will be no grade on the test and that they will correct their own papers. (Some teachers tell the class before they take the test that it will not be graded. This cuts down on cheating and testing panic. However, they may not try as hard if the test is not to be graded. Probably the best answer is to use both methods interchangeably.)

3.   Have a student give the answer to the first item. Ask the rest of the class if the answer is correct. If the class agrees, ask if anyone had a different answer. Discuss whether answers are correct, partly correct, or totally wrong. In the process, you are likely to receive criticism on how you worded your

question. If you didn't write it well, admit it, explain it, and go on. Go through all the items in the same way.

4. Get a rough estimate of how well the class did. Ask how many got all items correct, how many missed one, etc. Jot down the numbers on the chalkboard so the class can see the spread. Stop at 5 or 6 items—if you get a picture of how many did well, you also have a picture of how many did poorly. If few or none did well on the test, you have a problem either with how the lesson was taught or on how the test items were written. It is time to question the class to find out where the problem is.

5. If you want to pinpoint problems in the test or in your teaching, go down the test item by item and ask, "How many got this correct? How many missed this item?" Write the numbers on the board. The numbers can often give a clue about your teaching or about the test. If almost everyone missed an item, it is a good indicator that the class needs some review on that part of the lesson—or else it means that the test item was not clear.

VISUAL MEDIA

Most of us are visual learners. That means we learn better and faster by seeing something, instead of just being told about it. Consider the difference between looking at a set of building plans and having them described to you. When you get a picture, you get the picture. That's where visual aids come in handy.

Not all media are created equal however. Videos and slides are often of questionable quality, and can put your class and you to sleep. Transparencies, on the other hand, have many advantages over videos, DVDs, or slides. The lights stay on, your class stays awake, and you choose and control everything that is on the screen. Chapter 9 give you all the information you'll need about using transparencies and computer presentations, and it covers other visual media as well.

When you feel that a video, DVD, or slide sequence would be helpful, make sure you preview and choose your material carefully. Ask yourself if the information is presented clearly and accurately, and if it is truly time-efficient. If a film take twenty minutes to explain something that could just as easily be taught in ten, it's probably a waste of time.

Before you show your DVD or video, make sure the class knows what they are expected to learn. Then, stay put to make sure they are learning it. Do not leave while the video is running—if you don't stay with it, they won't stay with it.

SUMMARY

The presentation skills and the eleven teaching methods covered in this chapter give you a wide variety of ways to teach. Most teachers use a variety of these techniques according to their class, their subject, the setting, and their teaching style. A frequent change of pace will keep your class alert and actively involved in learning. Pay attention to your communication skills to make sure that your message gets through.

Chapter 5

NUTS AND BOLTS

MANAGING THE DETAILS

Your students will never notice many of the things you do to make the class operate. But dozens of details you decide on make the difference in how well your class works. Your class can run like a well-oiled machine or it can sputter along like a second-hand clunker.

Your most important decision is to have some well-thought-out plans **before you start teaching the class**.

This chapter is called "Nuts and Bolts" because it covers many of the details that make a class work well. It assumes that you have both a classroom and a shop or lab for hands-on projects like carpentry, computers, or electronics. If you have only a classroom, use the advice that applies to your own situation. Some of the suggestions in this chapter are related to teaching methods covered in the other chapters.

COURSE OUTLINES

A written **course outline** is a must. It gives you a road map that tells you where you are going. You should know exactly what you will teach on your last day of class before you even begin your first day of class. You can teach off the top of your head without a lesson plan once in a while and get away with it—if your conscience will allow you to settle for a poor job. But you can't start up a class without a course outline and get away with it.

A course outline lists what you plan to teach and the order in which you will teach it. It includes both class lessons and shop projects arranged in a logical teaching order. Remember that your teaching should be in short steps of instruction, and make sure the lessons—and especially the shop projects—advance from the simple to the complex. Always plan for practice and repetition.

Time Estimates

Once you have a tentative course outline written, estimate the amount of time that each lesson and project will take, and compare this to the teaching time you have available. You may find that you have to eliminate some of the lessons or projects you planned to teach. In general, it is better to teach less material thoroughly than to zip through too much too fast and risk leaving the class confused and discouraged.

Experienced teachers already know that a teaching hour and a clock hour don't take the same amount of time. Getting the class settled down, calling roll, handing out papers, discussing some event related to the class, coffee break, putting away tools and equipment, and cleaning the shop—all these take up time. In addition, you may have to conform to a public school class schedule in which a one-hour class is only 50 minutes long. (The other ten minutes is to allow students to walk from one class to another.) So in reality, a one-hour class may have only about 40 or 45 minutes of teaching time available—maybe less

This means that a 7:00 to 10:00 class is not three hours full of teaching—teaching time may be as short as two hours and 15 minutes. If you have a class that is officially scheduled for 144 hours per year, you may actually be teaching as little as 110 hours per year. So be realistic with your estimates of how much you can teach.

Evaluate you time and your goals to put together a course outline that really works. Make sure that your teaching goals can truly be reached in the hours, weeks, or months that you will be teaching.

LESSON PLANS

Teaching a class without a lesson plan is like building a house without plans or specs. Lesson plans are an essential part of planning a successful class. Lesson plans hep you work smarter instead of harder in two ways:

1. They guarantee that you will be more effective than you would if you taught off the top of your head.

2. They cut down on much of the preparation time that you would otherwise spend over subsequent years.

Chapter 6 has more detailed information on how to create an effective lesson plan, including a detailed sample lesson plan to use as a guideline for you own.

PROJECT PLANS

A project plan is a plan for teaching a shop project. In the shop or lab, because we know the material so well, we all tend to wing it. However, teaching off the top of the head is never the best job of teaching—it means doing a lot of repetitious work, and it may leave the student confused.

A project plan requires four things:

1. The list of projects from your course outline

2. A job sheet

3. Key questions

4. Evaluation standards

List of Projects

Keep a numbered list of projects in the front of the binder in which you store the project plans. The list of projects has three purposes:

1. You can check to see that you have covered all the skills you wish to.

2. You can see where a particular project fits in to the sequence of the projects.

3. Since the projects on the list are numbered, you can number job sheets to match.

Job Sheets

The **job sheet** is the key element of the project plan. It tells the student what must be done for a particular project.

A job sheet should give the specifications for the project, a drawing if necessary, and any information about the way in which the job should be done. Check the sample job sheet on the opposite page.

Of course, some projects are so simple that a job sheet isn't necessary. If you can show someone what to do and completely explain it in a sentence or two, a job sheet is probably not needed. On the other hand, if the students are constantly doing a project differently from the way you envisioned it, you need a job sheet.

A job sheet has three advantages over oral instructions alone:

- Each student is given the same instructions.
- You don't forget to explain important points.
- When you are pressed for time, you can give the student the job sheet and don't have to take time to explain the whole job orally.

Pg 59- 63-Chap 1

JOB SHEET 4

LAY OUT SOLE PLATES FOR SINGLE STORY BUILDING

I.   Tools and materials needed

    A.   Framing square

    B.   100 foot tape measure

    C.   Electric handsaw

    D.   Claw hammer

    E.   Pencil

    F.   Two 2 x 4's, 16ft. long, for plates

    G.   16d box nails

II.   Procedures

    A.   Select 2 x 4's from sixteen-foot stock for plates.

       NOTE: Crooked 2 x 4's may be used for the sole plates. They can easily be straightened as they are nailed to the floor, Good straight stock must be used for the top and double plate.

    B.   Cut the sole plate and top plate to length and tack to floor side by side with ends flush (see below).

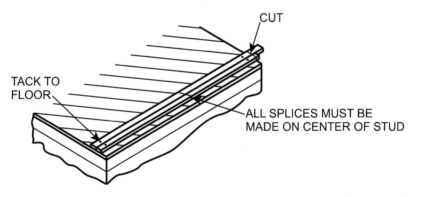

    C.   Lay out stud locations on plates doing side walls first and then walls. Lay out all walls from left to right.

       1. Mark plates for corner post (see below). Use the framing square with the blade held parallel to the edge of the plates and mark off.

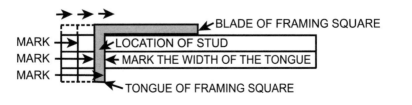

Key Questions and Evaluation Standards for Projects

Key questions are the questions to ask about a finished project in order to be sure the student really understands what was done. **Evaluation standards** are the things you want to check out on the finished project in order to assign a grade or score—or simply to give the student some helpful criticism.

Most key questions are standard items that apply to many different projects. For example, here are some **typical key questions**:

- Explain how you did this.

- Why did you do it (a certain way)?

- How did you determine (a measurement, mix proportions, size)?

- What will you do differently the next time you do this?

Evaluation standards also apply to many different jobs. For example, here are some **typical evaluation standards**:

- Project is square and plumb.

- Finish is professional quality.

- Matches specified dimensions.

- Performs according to specifications.

- Faulty equipment now performs correctly.

- Solves the problem specified.

Of course, you have key questions and evaluation standards in your head all the time. But if you make a list of your key questions, you can use it to be sure that you won't forget to ask important questions when you review a project. If you have a list of your evaluation standards, you can make sure that you evaluate all the projects by the same standards.

You will improve your teaching and evaluation tremendously if you have a list of key questions and a list of evaluation standards in the front of your binder—and use it. You may find that the very process of thinking them out and writing them down is the most valuable part of the process. After you use your lists for a while, you will stop referring to them because you will have them memorized.

Some projects will require special questions and standards. Put these on the job sheet. They are handy for you when you review the project, and they will help the student do a better job.

SEATING

You may not have any choice in how your classroom or your shop can be arranged. But if you do, give some thought to class seating and the shop arrangement.

Oddly enough, the seating arrangement in a classroom affects attitudes. A traditional classroom arrangement with rows of seats and a teacher's desk like a barrier between you and the class sets up a feeling of separation—perhaps even antagonism—between you and them. A circular seating arrangement with you sitting as part of the circle creates an open feeling that says, "We are all in this together." The class is much more likely to be open in their discussion.

You may not want to go with either one of these extremes of seating arrangements The fact is, you usually have to select a compromise arrangement. Everyone in class must be able to see the chalkboard. If you have drafting tables in the classroom, the seating possibilities are limited. If you set up a projector screen, everyone has to be able to see it.

Just remember that the seating arrangement affects the attitude of the class, and consider the best arrangement within your limitations.

RULES

You may think you won't need any rules. You may be wrong. Here are some good rules on rules:

- Have rules.

- Think out the consequences of a rule.

- Don't make rules you can't enforce—or don't want to enforce.

Clear, sensible rules help you to cope with or even avoid common classroom problems. They let the class know what is expected of them, and they ensure that everyone is treated in the same way.

Use common sense and be fair when you set up your rules. It simply makes sense to have rules about such things as lateness, absences, smoking, coffee breaks, and cleanup. These are all common sources of problems that can be avoided, or at least minimized, with simple clear-cut rules.

Always think out the consequences of your rules. A basic rule about rules is that people will find a way to break rules they don't like. Each new rule is likely to create new behavior in the class, so think out what that is likely to be. For example, if you rule that there will be no coffee breaks, they may bring thermoses of coffee into the lab and start to drink and visit while they work. If there is no smoking on school premises, they may walk off the grounds at coffee break time in order to smoke. Then you have the new problem of coffee breaks that take too long.

Every rule creates a problem of enforcement. If you don't or can't enforce some of your rules, you send the message that none of your rules need to be taken seriously. If you decide to make a rule that anyone who misses two nights of class will be suspended for a week, be sure your supervisor will back you on it. And think out whether you are going to back the rule if your favorite student is the first to break it.

Make sure your rules don't conflict with management. You may want to allow smoking or eating in class, but it may violate company or school policy.

Sometimes for difficult or touchy problems—such as smoking or no smoking—it helps to discuss the situation with the class. There are two approaches. One is to say. "Let's discuss this and vote on it." The second approach is to say, "Let's discuss this so that I can make a decision on it." This leaves you the option to make the final decision.

Finally, don't make more rules than you need to. They can make life complicated for you and irritating for your class.

ATTENDANCE AND GRADE RECORDS

Suppose you make a rule that two absences means a week's suspension from the job, and you have the backing to enforce this rule. You will set yourself up for a lot of trouble and turmoil unless you have complete, accurate records of attendance.

Keeping accurate records of attendance and grades will save you more problems than anything else you can do. You can't go to your supervisor and ask that a student be disciplined for non-attendance if you have no accurate record of attendance. You can't recommend that someone should not receive a training-related raise unless you have a record of poor attendance or poor grades. And your records have to be organized and complete for the whole class. If all you have are some scribbled scraps of paper, your records will be challenged.

Public schools often have attendance and grade record forms. If you can obtain these, they are usually well organized and complete. If these are not available, make you own forms. For each class you should have an **attendance record** and a **grade sheet**.

Be sure to include all the necessary data on your record sheets so that anyone reading them a year or so later can easily identity the class and the time. Details that are clear to you now will be forgotten in a few months. So write everything down. For example, the sample attendance record below has a key to the code for marking "present," and "late," and "absent." It is easy to forget exactly what code you used if you are asked to look up a student's record in a year or so.

Attendance Record

CODES
Present: ✓
Late: ＼
Absent: ✗

School __Central High__   Class __Cement Mason Appr__

School year __2005-06__   Section __First year__

Semester __Fall__   Day __9 - 8__

Instructor __John Jones__   Time __7 - 9 p.m.__

	Sept. 4	5	6	7	8	11	12	13	14
Bowman, Jeff	✓		✗		✓				
Mason, Cindy	✓		✓		✓				
Sanchez, Ray	＼		✓		✓				

Grade Sheet

School __Central High__   Class __Cement Mason Appr__

School year __2005-06__   Section __First year__

Semester __Fall__   Day __9 - 8__

Instructor __John Jones__   Time __7 - 9 p.m.__

	Orientation	Safety	History	Edge Forms	Finish Floors	Finish Roofs	Building Level	Screeds	
Bowman, Jeff	A	✓	B						
Mason, Cindy	C	✓	B						
Sanchez, Ray	B	✓	A						

64 - Top 6A Grap 2

It's a good idea to have a separate grade sheet. Combining the grades and attendance on the same sheet becomes messy and hard to read. Also, having the grade sheet under the attendance sheet provides more confidentiality for student grades.

PROGRESS CHART

Students like to know how they are progressing in the class. A progress chart (below) posted in the shop or lab shows them which projects they have completed and which they have to do. This chart is also an excellent way for you to see the progress of each student. Put a diagonal line to show that a project has been assigned and complete the X with a second diagonal line to show that the project was completed satisfactorily.

Don't use grades on a progress chart. This information should be kept between you and the individual. Also grades on the chart tend to make the class think in terms of grades instead of learning. If you are grading projects, put the grade on your grade sheet.

If there is any objection to posting progress information by name, you can use a code instead of a name. Some teachers assign a number to each student for posting grades or progress.

Progress Chart

Started \
Completed ✗

Cement Mason John Jones Fall 2005 - 06	Edge Forms	Finish Floors	Finish Roofs	Building Level	Screeds				
Bowman, Jeff	✗	✗	✗	\					
Mason, Cindy	✗	\							
Sanchez, Ray	✗	✗	\						

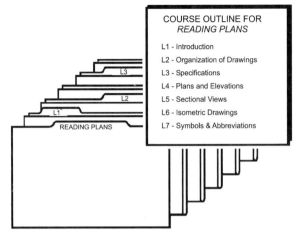

COURSE OUTLINE FOR
READING PLANS

L1 - Introduction
L2 - Organization of Drawings
L3 - Specifications
L4 - Plans and Elevations
L5 - Sectional Views
L6 - Isometric Drawings
L7 - Symbols & Abbreviations

STORING PAPERS

There is no point in keeping good records, lesson plans, and other materials unless you can find them when you need them.

Try to have file cabinet space available to you. Use it to store records, lesson plans, extra copies of quizzes and tests, and other class material. Set up a system for organizing your papers. You should be able to retrieve your papers months or years down the line. You will probably teach the same class again, or you may want to help someone else who will. Don't let the time you spend on paperwork be lost because you can't find your papers again.

The easiest system is to use your course outline and number each lesson (L1, L2, etc.) and each job project (P1, P2, etc.). Keep this marked outline in the front of the file drawer and mark and file all your course papers by this number.

For example, if you write a quiz for Lesson 1, type L1 in the upper corner of the original sheet of the quiz. Extra copies of the quiz are filed in a folder behind a file divider marked L1—as are all other class papers for lesson L1. When you need a certain paper, you don't have to try to remember what title you used for that subject. You simply look at the course outline, find the lesson number, and look under that number. This method also keeps together the papers you probably will need at a certain time.

While you are teaching a particular class, set up a binder with one set of all the papers you need for that class. This will include your attendance and grade sheets, course outline, and other records. Lesson plans, quizzes, assignment sheets, and other class materials can be arranged by lesson number. Job sheets can be arranged by project number. This will be a convenient way of keeping everything at hand and save time that might be spent in pulling papers from a filing cabinet. Extra copies of items such as quizzes and job sheets can be kept in the filing cabinet.

HOUSEKEEPING

Whether you teach in a classroom or a shop or lab, you need to take care of housekeeping. In a classroom—whether it's in a school building or a business conference room—you need to leave the room at least as neat as you found it. Make sure that the chalkboard is clean, chairs are back in place, and papers picked up. In short, leave it the way you expect to find it.

In a shop or lab, keeping track of tools and equipment and enforcing clean-up are two constant headaches. There are so many different situations that it is impossible to recommend any one system. Certain things hold true for every situation:

- You must have some kind of a system to be sure that all tools and instruments are back in their proper places and everything is clean before the class is dismissed. If you don't, you will spend your time picking up after the class, and—even worse—you will have disappearing tools.

- Whatever system you have, you must enforce it. Many people will not do their share of cleanup or tool return unless there is some pressure to do it.

If you are lucky enough to have a paid shop assistant, much of your problem is solved. However, most of us are not that lucky. You have to find what works best for you and your situation. All of these systems have been used successfully:

- Have an open equipment room so the students can take what they need. At the end of class, no one leaves until everything is back in its place and the shop is clean. This depends on having a clearly marked place for each item so that it is easy to check to see what is still missing. For example, you might be able to use a shadowboard, with the silhouette of each tool painted on the wall where it hangs. One problem with this system is that the responsible people do the pick-up and the deadbeats let them. Also, frequently you will have one tool still missing, and the class pressuring you to let them go anyway.

- Assign a student to be the equipment room manager. Students sign out for all equipment. The class is not dismissed until the equipment room manager reports that all items are in. Rotate the manager assignment.

- Require each trainee to bring basic hand tools or instruments. Class-supplied special tools and instruments will still be in the equipment room. An alternate to this is to provide each student with a tool box with basic tools. Each student is responsible to return the complete box and tools at the end of the class.

- For cleanup, give each one the responsibility for cleaning up one area or one item in the shop or lab. Make one student the foreman who has to see that each job is done properly. Rotate the assignments.

HANDLING MONEY

The best rule for handling money is DON'T! Not only is collecting money an interference with your teaching, but if it is lost you take the blame. If you are in a situation that requires collecting money for books or tools, first try to have the job done by some administrative office. If you must collect the money, buy a receipt book from a stationer's store and give each person a receipt for money received. Keep the money in a separate, secure container and turn it in as quickly as you can. Never leave it in the classroom overnight.

TIMING

Clock time and teaching time are different. You can easily fritter away the clock time until your teaching time is only 50% of an hour.

Class routines can dribble away your teaching time. But you can find many ways to save time. Try the following suggestions, but look for other time-savers as well:

- Don't hand out papers during class unless it is really necessary: it takes up time and distracts the class so that they won't be giving you their full attention. Instead, set out papers at the end of the class for the students to pick up.

- Calling roll is a good idea for the first few class meetings so that you can learn names, but you don't have to keep up the practice. Use a sign-in sheet or have a student check roll. Rotate the assignment.

Start on Time

All of us know someone who is always late. You learn to expect it. If you run late, your class will catch on fast. If they learn that you never get the 7:00 class started until 7:10. They will start arriving at 7:10—or even 7:15 or later. On the other hand, if your class always starts promptly at 7:00, they will be there and ready to start on time. If word gets around that you start right on the button and it is embarrassing to come in late, you will have gained several hours of teaching time over the year.

Maintain Coffee Break

Break time is important because it gives the class a change of pace. Most of us are more productive if we have a break. But it is easy for a fifteen minute coffee break to stretch to thirty minutes over the course of a year. Probably the only solution is to be aware of this and keep pounding at it whenever it starts to stretch out.

You can extend the break for some special occasion as long as it doesn't become a habit. If there is a good bull session going about a class-related problem, or if the students are talking to an interesting guest speaker, you may decide that more education is going on outside the classroom than you could achieve inside.

End on Time

Just as you expect the class to get there on time, they have a right to expect you to end on time.

Start shop or lab cleanup five or ten minutes (whatever your situation requires) before ending time so the class can leave on time. Usually, it is better to continue a lesson to the next class session rather than carry on for another fifteen minutes. This is not only a courtesy to the class but also good sense. People are tired and get restless and inattentive when quitting time comes around.

STUDENT RELATIONS

Remember that your students are individuals and each has different problems and each reacts differently to a situation. Work hard at getting to know them and their particular problems.

Some of your students may not thoroughly understand the language or the culture. Others may have physical disabilities to cope with. Workers who cannot read or do math will resort to some pretty weird behavior rather than admit to their problem. And of course, drugs and alcohol are frequent problems.

By yourself, you cannot remedy problems like these, but you may be able to get the student into a program that can. The community or employer may have resources. Drug and alcohol programs are probably available.

Check the community college, adult school, or library for literacy programs or language and math classes. Some companies make an arrangement with the local community college to have basic skills classes taught on site.

You probably can't require your students to get the help you think they need. But you can talk to them—privately!—to let them know what help is available and encourage them to make use of it.

Just remember that you are not an expert in diagnosing problems and your students are likely to resent what they take as criticism. Tread lightly. Never embarrass them in public. If you think a student has a problem you can talk about, see that person privately.

The Three Fs

The 3 Fs of teaching are Fair, Firm, and Friendly.

Being **fair** means that you must conduct your class by reasonable rules and that you must treat all students by the same standards and with the same respect. It's tough to be equally fair to the aggressive know-it-all who annoys you and the cheerful clown everyone loves. Fairness requires another tough task of you—sometimes admitting that you were wrong and the class was right.

Being **firm** means making your class rules and sticking by them. Don't let the class con you out of them. The great trick here is to make class rules that you are willing to enforce. Don't paint yourself into a corner. Leave room for exceptions—there will always be some.

For example, suppose you make the rule that anyone who misses three nights of class is dropped—no exceptions. Sure as shooting, the first one who misses three nights is your best student who has to go out of town on a job. Of course you say that is a good reason and you work it out. But it makes you look foolish and it tells the class that your absolute rules are not all that absolute.

Being **friendly** means that you cannot be an ironfisted dictator and get the best out of your class—but neither can you be too chummy. The best learning occurs when the teacher truly enjoys the class, the class likes the teacher, and there is a relaxed enjoyable atmosphere in the classroom or shop. The teacher is friendly, but clearly in charge.

You can determine how informal you want to be. Let your class know how to address you—whether it should be Mr. or Mrs. or Ms. Or a first name. Decide if you will call your students by first names or last names. I have found that the title the students use to address the teacher has little to do with their attitude towards the teacher. Respect is earned (not mandated) by the manner in which you conduct your class and by your behavior as the teacher and leader. Remember the 3 Fs!

When I used to visit vocational classes to evaluate the instructors, the relationship between the instructor and the students told me as much as seeing the actual teaching performance. It the class was running well, the atmosphere was often informal and there was a lot of kidding going on—with the teacher receiving much of it. But it was easy to see that they respected and like the teacher—and that the teacher was in charge and was seeing to it that learning was taking place.

p 73 Timin - 76 Grap 4

Chapter 6

WORKING SMART

THE LESSON PLAN

After forty years of being involved in almost every part of teaching and teacher training, I will say flat out that you are pretty dumb if you don't start using lesson plans. I taught for almost ten years before I wised up and realized what a time saver they are, and how much better and easier it makes teaching.

A **lesson plan** is a carefully thought out and written strategy for teaching a lesson. A lesson plan makes the difference between one year's experience ten times, and ten years of fruitful experience.

If you are already using lesson plans, this chapter should give you some new ideas for improving your plans. If you are not using lesson plans, here is your chance to get smart and learn to cut down your work and improve your teaching.

Teaching in the lab or shop also needs a plan, but your project plan will be in the form of job sheets, key questions, and evaluation standards, as covered in Chapter 5, Nuts and Bolts.

LESSON LENGTH

There is much more to a lesson than just handing out some facts. One key to a good lesson is to plan short steps of instruction.

The length of a lesson is somewhat determined by the schedule of your class. For most classes, 50 minute lessons work well. This takes up one class hour. If you have a two-hour class, you can use two different lessons. Some lessons will take much more than an hour even though they are the proper short steps of instruction. Math lessons, for example, often require more than an hour because the class needs time to work problems, correct them, and rework more problems.

If you have a three-hour class that includes lab work, 50 minute lessons still work well, because you can have an hour of class and still have two hours left for lab work.

REASONS FOR LESSON PLANS

Lesson plans are so important that many schools require their teachers to have lesson plans prepared ahead of time and on file in the office. Having a prepared lesson plan makes it possible for a substitute teacher to take over.

Having a lesson plan saves you a lot of time, because once you have the plan, you are ready to teach the class again at any time. You don't have to repeat the preparation time.

Even more important, a lesson plan allows you to teach the class at your peak potential. You'll do a good job the first time you use it. Even better, you can add notes and make improvements in the plan each time you teach from it, so your teaching will get better every time you teach the same subject again.

You'll earn the respect of your students if you give them a well planned class with all the materials you need at hand. Nothing makes a teacher look bad faster than fumbling around for missing materials or stumbling over words because the lesson isn't prepared. Having a lesson plan means that your classes will go smoothly. You'll feel good about them.

Lesson planning provides the following benefits:

- It forces you to analyze what you will teach.

- It forces you to organize what you teach.

- It ensures that all material and equipment will be ready for the lesson.

- It helps you choose the most effective methods of teaching that particular lesson.

- It makes sure that you will not forget to mention some important point in the lesson.

- If you are teaching more than one class on the same subject, it lets you know that you will teach all classes in the same way and equally well.

- The next time you teach this lesson—even if it is a year later—you have a written record of what you taught. Most of your preparation for the lesson is already done for you. All you have to do is review your plan and your notes.

- By adding notes for improvement immediately after teaching the lesson, you will be able to improve your teaching the next time you teach it.

CONTENT OF THE LESSON PLAN

Every instructor who wants to improve will probably change lesson plan forms several times before settling on exactly the right format. If you are already using a satisfactory lesson plan form, you may find some new ideas in this chapter to improve it.

If you are not using any lesson plan, use the format we present here as a starting point and gradually change it as you see ways to improve it to fit your teaching situation.

A lesson plan should contain at least the following:

1. Course title

2. Lesson title

3. Estimated time needed for the lesson

4. Objectives of the lesson

5. Materials needed for the lesson
   A.   For demonstrations
   B.   For media (projectors, slides, DVDs, etc.)
   C.   For class handouts (tests, quizzes, job sheets)
   D.   For special materials needed for the lesson
   E.   For shop or lab work

6. Outline of the lesson

7. Assignments

8. Notes (such as actual time used on lesson, notes for improvement the next time, questions to ask, problems to avoid, etc.)

Generally lesson plans should be one or two pages long. If they are too long, they get awkward to handle and you won't use them.

The outline of the lesson may be very detailed or very brief, depending on what works best for you. For a subject you know very well, all you need are the key points you wish to cover. For a subject that you are not as familiar with, you may want to have a more detailed outline.

ORGANIZING LESSON PLANS

You will never develop and use lesson plans unless you set up a system for storing and retrieving them easily. The simplest way is to set up a binder or portable file with divider tabs. I recommend giving each lesson a number (L1, L2, etc.) and labeling the divider tabs with these lesson numbers. Keep a course outline in the front of the binder or file in order to quickly find the name of lesson L1 or L2. You could also label the tabs by lesson title or by subject (such as Basic Electricity, Ohm's Law, Parallel Circuits). You can apply this same format to your computer files.

The important thing is that you set up some way so that you can quickly put your hands on the lesson plan you want. If something is hard to locate, human nature being what it is, we tend to not use it.

There is another advantage to having your lesson plans together in a binder. You can easily make a last minute change if you have to. For example, you may decide that your class is not ready for the lesson you had prepared. Or you may find that some materials you need are not available. Perhaps your lab is not available to work in and you have to use the classroom. If you have other lesson plans on hand, you can easily switch to a different lesson on short notice. You may want to have some lesson plans especially designed to use on short notice if necessary.

The first sheet in your lesson plan binder should be a sample format for your lesson plan, similar to the one on the next page. This makes sure that all of your lesson plans will be organized in the same way. You will refer to it when you start to write a new plan. If you have someone keyboard your lesson plan, make sure that person has a sample format sheet so that all of your lesson plans have the same format.

Having the same format for all your lesson plans is more than just fussiness. It is easier to find and use items you are looking for if all the sheets are in the same style and use the same headings.

WRITING LESSON PLANS

Here's a good system to follow when writing your lesson plans:

1. Write the objectives of the lesson.
2. Outline the presentation.
3. Outline the introduction.
4. Outline the application.
5. Plan the test.
6. Fill in the headings for the lesson plan sheet.

LESSON PLAN

COURSE:_____ INSTRUCTOR: _____

LESSON TITLE:_____ DATE:_____

TIME NEEDED FOR THE LESSON: _____

OBJECTIVES

MATERIALS NEEDED

INTRODUCTION

PRESENTATION

TEST

ASSIGNMENT

NOTES

Lesson plan format: The amount of space between headings will vary according to your lesson plan. This format is easy to use on the computer.

Let's say right at the start that the sample lesson plan at the end of this chapter is probably more detailed than you generally will need. We had to do this so that you could see what we intended to show. At the same time, recognize that you should put in more detail than you think necessary. Remember that after you teach the lesson plan, you may not use it again for several months or even until next year. The things that were clear now may not be so clear then unless you write them out in sufficient detail.

WRITE THE OBJECTIVES

Write the objectives first to clarify your thinking. It helps you define the limits and direction of the lesson. For example, consider these three statements of objectives written for the same lesson:

OBJECTIVE A

Students will be able to calculate cubic feet and cubic yards.

OBJECTIVE B

Students will be able to:

1. Write the equation for calculating the volume of a cube.
2. Explain how the equation was derived.

OBJECTIVE C

Students will be able to:

1. Write the equation, from memory, for calculating the volume of a rectangular solid.
2. Calculate the cubic feet or cubic yards of any rectangular solid when given the dimensions in feet and inches.

Even though they all describe the same subject, these objectives would result in three entirely different lessons. Let's take a look at each one and see how it would work.

> ## OBJECTIVE A
>
> Students will be able to calculate cubic feet and cubic yards.

Objective A is vague and allows the lesson to wander. As written, it means that the student must be able to calculate the volume of any kind of a solid object (cube, prism, sphere, etc.). It does not give any starting basis. Does the student have to remember the equation or not? Does the student have to calculate cubic feet if given metric dimensions?

Having a vague objective means you haven't really defined what you plan to teach.

> ## OBJECTIVE B
>
> Students will be able to:
>
> 1. Write the equation for calculating the volume of a cube.
> 2. Explain how the equation was derived.

Objective B may be what a math teacher would want to teach, but it's not what a trade teacher would want to teach. Calculating the volume of a cube is too limiting, because the actual shapes that people on the job have to deal with are usually not perfect cubes. In addition, they have to be able to use the equation, not explain how it is derived. Objective B states legitimate objectives for a certain type of math course—but not for workers on the job.

> ## OBJECTIVE C
>
> Students will be able to:
> 1. Write the equation, from memory, for calculating the volume of a rectangular solid.
> 2. Calculate the cubic feet or cubic yards of any rectangular solid when given the dimensions in feet and inches.

We will use Objective C as a guide for the lesson plan. It is more in keeping with teaching practical applications that most people need. It is specific enough to guide your teaching.

Objectives define what you are going to teach. Vague objectives like Objective A permit you to wander all over with no specific direction to your lesson. Objectives B would take your lesson in a different direction from Objective C.

OUTLINE THE PRESENTATION

Notice that the Introduction Step is not the first step you plan. This is because the Objectives and the Presentation are really the meat of the lesson. Once these two are determined, the rest of the lesson hangs on them.

The "outline" of the presentation doesn't have to be a formal outline. It can be a list of notes, in the proper order, that will remind you what you want to do. You probably know the subject so well that you really don't need notes to tell you what to say. But you do need something to make sure that an important point does not slip your mind.

Here is one way to outline your presentation:

1. Write down the **new** skills and knowledge that the class will need to achieve the objectives.
2. Check to see if all these items really fit in this lesson.
3. Arrange the remaining items in the best order for teaching.
4. Under each of these, fill in how you will teach them.

For example, for Objective C you could list the skills and knowledge that the class needs like this:

1. The equation for figuring the volume of a rectangular solid

2. Define: rectangular solid, volume, cubic feet, cubic yards
3. Changing feet to yards
4. Changing cubic feet to cubic yards
5. Changing cubic yards to cubic feet
6. Changing inches to decimals of a foot
7. Using the proper units of measurement

Of course, there are many other abilities that the students must have, such as how to multiply, and understanding feet and inches. These are not listed because you know that these have been taught in previous lessons or you assume these skills as basic requirements for entering the class. The next step is to examine the list to see if it is appropriate for one lesson. This is a matter of your judgment on how well your class does in math and how much is too much.

Let's assume that, after checking this list, you decide that your class already understands the principles of using the proper units of measurement and that item 7 can be deleted. In addition, you decide that, for this class at least, the lesson contains too many things for the class to absorb at once. Therefore you decide to make items 4 and 5 (changing back and forth between cubic feet and cubic yards) a separate lesson. (Remember—short steps of learning.) The list for the lesson would now look like this:

1. The equation for figuring the volume of a rectangular solid
2. Define: rectangular solid, volume, cubic feet, cubic yards
3. Changing feet to yards
4. Changing inches to decimals of a foot

Now arrange the list in the best order for teaching. It seems logical that definitions (item 2) would come first. It is probably smart to give the equation next and have the class use it with simple numbers. Then by giving the class a measurement in feet and inches, they will see the need for being able to change feet and inches into yards. Therefore, the basic outline for your presentation is this:

1. Define: rectangular solid, volume, cubic feet, cubic yards
2. The equation for figuring the volume of a rectangular solid
3. Changing feet to yards
4. Changing inches to decimals of a foot

Now you are ready to decide how to teach these ideas to the class. Under each item, list the things you will do and the points you want to cover. For example, the outline for the first point could look like this:

1. Define: rectangular solid, volume, cubic feet, cubic yards
   a. What does volume mean?
      Amount of space occupied by a three-dimensional figure.
   b. Show some blocks of wood, a prism, and a ball.
      1) All are three dimensional figures.
      2) These are all called solids. Give their names.
      3) Each has a different equation for figuring the volume. We are concerned only with rectangular solids (write name on board).
      4) Draw rectangle on the board. Emphasize 90° corners. Extend sides to make a rectangular solid.
   c. Draw cube on board and dimension all the sides with 1. Explain cubic inches, feet, and yards. What if the 1 is one meter? What if it is a centimeter?

OUTLINE THE INTRODUCTION

Now that the objectives and the outline of the presentation are completed, it is easier to think of an introduction. You can probably think of several ways to do this. One method is by asking the class how to calculate materials. This could result in an introduction outline like this:

1. Ask the class these:

    a. Show a rectangular container. "Does this hold one gallon of water? Let's calculate to find out." Measure the container. There are 0.134 cubic feet in a gallon. How many gallons does this container hold?

    b. I have a garden bed that is 6" deep, 13'-5" long and 6'-7" wide. How many cubic yards of dirt are needed to fill it? (1.6 cu. yds.)

    c. A concrete form is 8½" wide, 1'-3" deep, and 32'-6" long. How many cubic yards of concrete will be needed to fill it? (1.07 cu. yds.)

2. Have everyone calculate the problems and see if anyone got the right answer.

3. For those of you who did not get the right answer, this unit will show you how to do it. For those who worked the problem correctly, this unit will show you better ways to do it. (Use any students who are able to do the problems as assistants later on in the lesson.)

4. Ask students for ways they need this skill on their job.

OUTLINE THE APPLICATION

The application is largely determined by the objectives and by the presentation. In this case, application was built into the presentation in several places because the students were required to make calculations. However, more application of practical problems on calculating material should be added. The Application Step would look something like this:

1. Write problems on board and have the class work them. Give dimensions in feet and inches.
2. Correct and discuss problems as each is done.

PLAN THE TEST

In this case, the best test is simply to see if the students can work practical problems without help. Therefore, you need a quiz for this lesson. The Test Step for this lesson plan would be very brief and could be noted like this:

Use Quiz 23. Collect and grade.

FILL IN THE HEADINGS

Filling out the rest of the lesson plan is routine. When you list the materials needed, be sure to check all the different steps carefully to be sure everything is covered.

The final, complete Lesson Plan would look like the sample that follows.

LESSON PLAN

COURSE: Trainee II   **INSTRUCTOR**: John Smith

LESSON TITLE: 23. Volume of a Rectangular Solid   **DATE**:

TIME NEEDED FOR THE LESSON: 2 hours

OBJECTIVES
Students will be able to:
1. Write the equation, from memory, for calculating the volume of a rectangular solid.

2. Calculate the cubic feet or cubic yards of any rectangular solid when given the dimensions in feet and inches.

MATERIALS NEEDED
1. Examples of solids (prism, ball, and several rectangular solids)

2. Quiz 23

3. Problem Sheet 23

INTRODUCTION

1. Ask the class these:
   a. Show a rectangular container. "Does this hold one gallon of water? Let's calculate to find out." Measure the container. There are 0.134 cubic feet in a gallon. How many gallons does this container hold?
   b. I have a garden bed that is 6" deep, 13'-5" long and 6'-7" wide. How many cubic yards of dirt are needed to fill it? (1.6 cu. yds.)
   c. A concrete form is 8½" wide, 1'-3" deep, and 32'-6" long. How many cubic yards of concrete will be needed to fill it? (1.07 cu. yds.)

2. Have everyone calculate the problems and see if anyone got the right answer.

3. For those of you who did not get the right answer, this unit will show you how to do it. For those who worked the problem correctly, this unit will show you better ways to do it. (Use any students who are able to do the problems as assistants later on in the lesson.)

4. Ask students for ways they need this skill on their job.

PRESENTATION

1. Define: rectangular solid, volume, cubic feet, cubic yards
   a. What does volume mean?
      (Amount of space occupied by a three-dimensional figure.)
   b. Show some blocks of wood, a prism, and a ball.
      1) All are three dimensional figures.
      2) These are all called solids. Give their names.
      3) Each has a different equation for figuring the volume. We are concerned only with rectangular solids (write name on board).
      4) Draw rectangle on the board. Emphasize 90° corners. Extend sides to make a rectangular solid.
   c. Draw cube on board and dimension all the sides with 1. Explain cubic inches, feet, and yards. What if the 1 was one meter? What if it was a centimeter?

2. Give equation for rectangular solid.
   a. Draw solid on board. Write in length, width, height.
   b. Write equation on board: Volume = Length x Width x Height.
      Write abbreviation of equation on board: V = L x W x H. Have class write this in their notebooks.
   c. Write in 2 on each dimension. Have someone tell what the volume is. Ask, "8 what?" Get class to say that the 2 must be stated in cubic inches, feet, or yards.
   d. Write in different dimensions (feet, inches, yards) and have the class calculate volume. Use rectangles as well as cubes. Don't mix feet and inches.
   e. Give quiz and self-correct. Check results with a show of hands. Handle any misunderstandings.

3. Changing feet to yards
   a. To get cubic yards, you have to start with yard dimensions.
      1) What do you do if you have dimensions in feet and you want cubic yards?
      2) How do you change feet into yards? How do you change cubic feet to cubic yards? Get them to understand that you have to divide by 27.
   b. Write dimensions in feet on the board and ask class to convert them to yards.

4. Changing feet and inches to feet only
    a. Write dimensions in feet and inches on the board.
       What do you do if you need cubic yards and the dimensions are in feet and inches? If any student can work it correctly, ask for an explanation. By questions, get all the class to these step-by-step conclusions:
        1) We need the dimensions in feet only.
        2) We can do this by changing the inches to decimals of a foot.
        3) There are 12″ in a foot.
        4) Divide inches by 12 to get decimals of a foot.
        5) Turn fraction of an inch to a decimal before dividing by 12.
    b. Write feet and inches on board and have the class convert to decimals.

APPLICATION

1. Write problems from Problem Sheet 23 on board and have the class work them. Give dimensions in feet and inches.

2. Correct and discuss problems as each is done.

TEST

1. Use Quiz 23. Collect and grade.

ASSIGNMENT

1. Read: Herberger, pp. 234-238, elementary geometric shapes

NOTES

Chapter 7

DID I TEACH?

WHY, WHAT, AND HOW TO TEST

Everyone hates taking tests—including your students. The pressure to do a good job and the fear of failure create a lot of anxiety. It's no picnic for teachers either. Many teachers would be happy to do away with testing—constructing tests, grading papers, and recording grades can be dull and tedious chores.

However, testing isn't such an awful chore if you know exactly why you are testing and know what kind of test to use for various purposes. This chapter has many practical tips that can make testing a lot easier for you.

REASONS FOR TESTING

Ask any student what tests are for and the answer will be immediate—grades. True enough—but that's only one of the reasons. Tests serve other purposes as well:

- To check their learning

- To check your teaching

- To motivate students

- To give grades

Test to Check Their Learning

The most important reason to test is to find out what has been learned—and what hasn't. You may be doling out lots of valuable information to your class, but if they aren't learning it, you're wasting your time, and theirs.

Testing will show you how much the class as a whole is learning and how much each individual is learning. You might discover that the class as a whole is excelling in one area but floundering in another. You might find that there is a wide range from your best student to your worst. Or you might discover that while most of them are making great progress, one or two are straggling far behind. You might get hints of all of this from in-class performance or from talking to your students, but through testing you can really find out exactly how everyone in your class is coming along.

You need to know how well your class is learning—and your class needs to know as well. They need feedback. Not just a pat on the back or a good word now and then, but the specific information that they get from reviewing their own test performance. They too need to know exactly how they're coming along.

Students need to be reassured that they are on track and on schedule. They also need to know if they aren't. The wake-up call of a low test score can motivate them to get back on track with the rest of the class.

Test to Check Your Teaching

Testing shows how well the students learned, AND it also shows how well the teacher taught. That's something you should be very interested in.

If most of your class does very badly on a test, you might assume they are all lazy and stupid. Perhaps they are. On the other hand, it may be that you didn't teach as effectively as you should have. That's why it's a good idea to use testing to check up on yourself. Remember—if the student hasn't learned, the teacher hasn't taught.

If the results of a test are poor, it may not be easy to determine immediately what needs improvement—the learning or the teaching or the test. Perhaps all three do. Check your teaching first to see if you need to make some changes. If the whole class is struggling in one particular area, it may be that your teaching on that particular point was not clear enough.

Test to Motivate Review

When did you do most of your review and studying when you were in school? Probably before a test. Most students study regular lessons just enough to keep up in class. But if a big test is coming up, they really hit the books. Cramming isn't the best way to learn, but at least it's learning. A test can be a great motivator when your students need a little extra push.

Testing at regular intervals can help your students to stay on track, learning and reviewing their lessons as they go along.

Test to Give Grades

Finally, you may have to give tests because you have to give grades. Naturally you need to plan your tests carefully to make sure that every test produces a fair way of assigning grades.

The rest of this chapter and Chapter 8 give you many practical pointers for making tests that are fair to your students, and easy for you and your class to use.

DECIDE WHAT YOU ARE TESTING FOR

You have to decide not only why you test but also what you test.

First of all, your course outline should tell you generally what the class needs to know when the course is completed. If learning how to make miter cuts is listed on the course outline, you probably ought to be testing that. Simply put, make sure you teach everything required, and make sure you test everything required. Other material may come up during your class time, but you don't have to test it if it isn't required.

Next, you have to decide what the students are expected to do with what they learn. You can ask them to use what they learn in one of four different ways:

- Recall it.

- Recognize it.

- Solve a problem with it.

- Perform a task with it.

Recall

Recall is the same as memorization. The students are expected to know and remember much of what they learn without any prompting.

Recognition

Some information can be recognized even if it isn't memorized. For example, if you were asked to list all the different tools used in your work, you might have some trouble remembering them all. But if you were given a list of many different tools you could easily pick out the tools used in your work. You know them when you see them and when you need them. That's recognition.

Problem Solving

Recall and recognition check on what the students know—problem solving shows you if they know how to use that knowledge. Problem solving can involve pure math problems, or word problems based on realistic on-the-job problems. For example, you could give the dimensions of a room and the square feet a quart of paint will cover, then ask the class to calculate the amount of paint needed.

Performance

A performance test asks the student to demonstrate skills by performing a certain task. Usually this is a hands-on test, not a paper and pencil test. However, a written test that demonstrates the ability to use math is also a performance test.

Don't use a written test as a substitute for a performance test. Many students can perform a task perfectly, but cannot tell you in writing how they do it. On the other hand, some can explain how to do something but may not be able to perform well. If you are testing for performance, it doesn't really matter how well they write about it—what matters is how they do the job. For example, don't ask the class to just list the steps for tuning up a motor. Give them a motor and have them DO the tune-up.

KEEP TESTS FAIR AND OBJECTIVE

The process of grading a test can be either objective or subjective. When you test and grade, you want to be as objective as possible, but you can't avoid some subjective judgments.

An **objective test** has answers that are either right or wrong, so there is no room for making judgments. Your personal opinion of what an individual deserves doesn't color the results of a purely objective test. You cannot be accused of being unfair to any individual if you are using a test that is entirely objective.

A **subjective test** requires you to make judgments. Not every question can be answered with a clear-cut, black-or-white answer. Sometimes it's a judgment call, and you are the judge. Your students expect you to be fair. And you expect to be fair. However, no matter how fair you try to be, if you are using your own judgment, you may be influenced by what you think of a particular person.

For the sake of your students, you want to be objective. They should be judged on their performance, not their personalities.

For your own sake, you want to be objective. If your grading is largely subjective, you may find that someone will challenge your fairness and your grades. In addition, an objective test with answers that are either right or wrong is easy to grade quickly. A subjective test that requires you to make a lot of individual decisions can take much more of your time to grade.

Judging hands-on projects and performance tends to be at least partly subjective. However, you can set up a rating system to make these as objective as possible. Written tests can be either objective or subjective. Design them to be as objective as possible.

THREE WAYS TO TEST

When you think of testing, you usually think of anxious students chewing their pencils and staring at test papers. That's a written test. There are actually three different ways to test:

- Oral test
- Performance test
- Written test

Oral

Oral questions should be used routinely in both classroom and shop teaching, but they can also be used for testing. They are especially useful for those who don't read very well. Oral questions are used mostly to test recall, but they can also test recognition or problem-solving.

When you ask questions in class as you teach, you are doing informal testing. The questions give you some idea of how well each person is keeping up with the class material. Direct your questions to individuals most of the time, because if you just ask volunteers to answer, the same ones will always do the talking.

Oral questions can also be used for a more formal kind of test. If you want to give an oral test, write out a list of questions ahead of time. Arrange to see each student separately, ask each of the questions, and record the responses. This is time-consuming, but it can often be done while other students are working on hands-on projects.

An oral test is not as objective as a written test. It is easy to favor someone you like, unconsciously giving clues to the answer you expect. If you are using the test for a grade, be careful to keep it as objective as possible so that everyone in class has an equal chance to succeed.

An oral test should follow these guidelines:

1. Have the questions written down so that you ask the same questions in the same way of everyone.

2. Record their responses so that you have a record of which questions were answered correctly.

Performance Test

A performance test involves doing a hand-on project that demonstrates a particular skill. This is a very useful kind of test, but it can be unfairly subjective.

To set up a valid performance test, see to it that everyone has to complete the same kind of project. They should all have the same tools, the same materials, and the same working conditions. Use a job sheet to establish the specifications for the project to be completed.

You should also set up a rating sheet so that the projects are graded as objectively as possible. The sheet should list qualities you will grade, assigning the percentage of the total score that each one can earn. The rating sheet can include items such as economical use of material or proper use of tools.

A performance test should follow these guidelines:

1. Write up a job sheet with clear-cut specs so that everyone knows exactly what has to be done and how it has to be done.

2. Write up a rating sheet listing the qualities or standards you will be judging. Assign a percentage of the total score to each one.

Written Test

A written test is the most objective kind of test and is the easiest to administer. Written test items usually test recall and recognition.

There are eight common types of test items:

- True/False

- Matching

- Multiple choice

- Completion

- Identification

- Math

- Short answer

- Essay

These eight different types of written tests are covered in detail in Chapter 8. The advantages and limitations of each are explained and examples are given.

Though a written test is easy to administer, it is not always easy to write really good test items. A question or instruction that may seem perfectly clear to you when you write might be completely misunderstood by your students.

To make sure that a written test is not frustrating for you or for your class, take enough time to make up a test carefully. Revising and double-checking your test takes time, of course. But if you skip it, be prepared to deal with questions, complaints, and squabbles over possible alternate answers. If a item does cause misunderstanding, be sure to change or replace it before you use the test again.

To avoid many frustrations small and large, observe the guidelines for constructing and using written tests covered in Chapter 8. Once you have well-constructed test items, you can save yourself a lot of time in the future by using these items in different combinations in future tests.

If some of your students have poor reading skills, they will do badly on a written test whether they know the material or not. You may have to make special arrangements for someone with a reading problem. Sometimes they just need a little extra time, but in more extreme cases, you may have to give the test orally.

MAKING THE GRADE

Grading tests fairly is always a challenge. It can be difficult to decide what scores earn an A, what scores earn a B, and so on. Then, too, you may find that some do well on performance tests but poorly on written tests. A final grade has to balance both.

Research has shown that whenever a large number of people are tested for any ability, a chart showing how the scores are distributed forms a characteristic shape called a **bell curve** or normal distribution curve. This curve shows that for any kind of test, most will score in the large middle range. A small number will score way above the middle range, and a small number will score way below it.

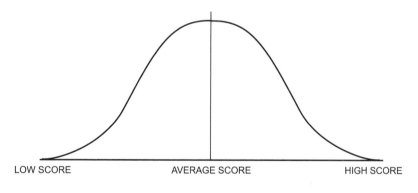

| LOW SCORE | AVERAGE SCORE | HIGH SCORE |

The bell curve shows the normal distribution of scores for any test if a large number of people are tested.

A single class is too small a group to form a bell curve. However, you will probably have a somewhat similar range: Most will be in the large middle group, but a few will lag behind or move ahead of the group.

Grading scales are often based on the bell curve. The large number in the middle earn a C and small numbers at each end earn an A or an F. Of course, a standard spread of grades works out accurately only with a large number of general students.

Your class will vary from the perfect bell curve because it is too small a sample. It will also vary for another reason—in adult classes the students choose to be there. Those who would do very badly in such a class probably will not choose to be there. That means that **you will probably not have the very lowest scores that would be expected according to the bell curve**.

This information on the bell curve is primarily a reminder that you can't expect all your students to perform at the same level. You are bound to have a normal amount of variation in your class. You have to teach to the whole range of students and you have to assign fair grades to the whole range.

A typical grading scale based on the bell curve uses the following percentages:

A — 8%

B — 17%

C — 50%

D — 17%

F — 8%

The range is intended as a general guide only. These particular percentages are just one grading system. You may choose to set up another grade range. Even more important, remember that **one class will not fit the range perfectly**. Someone who is a top performer in one class, may be only average if they happen to get thrown in with a more experienced group. The average level of each class is going to vary from group to group. You probably won't have too many students in the very lowest range, so you might want to keep that percentage pretty small.

To keep your grading fair to everyone in your class, follow these grading guidelines.

Don't assign a letter grade to a raw score before you have scored a whole batch of tests.

A raw score is the number of items correct. Suppose you decide ahead of time that on a 100-point test, a score of 90 to 100 will earn an A, 80 to 90 will earn a B, etc. Then when you grade the tests, you may find the test was so easy that everyone got A's and B's. On the other hand, if the test was difficult, they may all get D's and F's. Probably neither set of grades would be fair.

Instead, wait until after you have corrected and scored all the tests. Then you can determine fairly easily what range earns A, what earns B, etc. Use the following procedure to set a grade range.

First, write all the scores in numerical order. If you use the grading range listed above, about 8% of the top of the range should be A's. The next 17% should be B's. Then 50% are C's, 17% are D's, and 8% are F's. Divide your range of scores roughly according to these percentages. (You might decide there is a lower percentage of D's and F's.)

Be careful to temper your grading with common sense. Avoid making the cut-off between A and B a difference of one point; try to find a natural gap of several points to use as a cut-off. If there is no obvious spread in the low scores, you may not assign any F's or D's.

Remember that you can't expect your class to form a perfect bell curve. Use grading percentages only as a general guide.

You can avoid giving letter grades until the end of the term.

Some teachers don't give letter grades until the end of the term. They keep track of raw scores, add them up at the end of the term, and assign a letter grade according to the final raw scores. However, if you do this, you still have to let the students know how they are doing along the way. It wouldn't be fair at the end of the term to slap an F on students who had no idea that they were so far behind.

To avoid this problem without giving letter grades, let the class know what the range of raw scores is on every test. If the range is from 42 to 78, the guy with a score of 45 knows he is in trouble. The shock may cause those with low scores to pay more attention and study harder.

Not every test has the same value.

You can't just average all the scores during a term to determine a final grade. A ten-point quiz covering a single lesson shouldn't have as much value as a 100-point test at the end of the term. A major hands-on project may have more weight than a quiz. You have to decide how much each score is worth and set up a formula to calculate each final grade.

If a test has faulty items, throw them out.

Because it is difficult to construct a perfect test, you may find that one or two of your test items are faulty for some reason. If some misunderstood an item because of the way it was written, remove the item from the test before you assign grades.

Be as objective as you can be in assigning grades.

Make your written tests as objective and fair as possible. Set up a rating sheet for performance tests, and set up a record of answers for an oral test. You won't often have to make allowances for special cases if you have made sure that your testing methods are as fair and objective as you can make them.

SUMMARY

Before you give a test, be sure you know why you are giving the test and what you are testing for. Decide whether your test should be an oral test, a performance test, or a written test. Make the test as objective as possible. Grade fairly.

It's still no picnic, but if you plan carefully, testing can cause a minimum of fear and frustration for you and for your students.

Chapter 8

GARBAGE IN—GARBAGE OUT

WRITING TEST ITEMS

Constructing a good written test takes careful planning. Putting together 50 or 100 questions is hard enough. Making sure they test what you want to test for requires skill and knowledge. This chapter covers guidelines for constructing tests along with specific advantages, disadvantages, and limitations of eight different kinds of test items.

A quiz for a single lesson can be short and simple. A test to cover several lessons will probably be longer and include a mix of types of test items. Choose the kind of test items that fits your purpose.

Make your test as fair as possible. It should only test the material you want it to test. It should not be a test of reading or writing ability (unless you want to test for that). It should not favor some students more than others.

CONSTRUCTING A TEST

Test items are the basic building blocks of tests. If you construct a test covering several lessons, you will probably want to use about 100 test items. They should not be all the same kind of item; use a combination of different types, such as short answer and multiple choice. If the types of items are varied, the test will be less tedious for you to construct and for the class to take. A variety of items also helps you test for a variety of abilities such as recall, recognition, and the ability to work problems.

When you put the test together, keep similar items together in sections. For example, keep all the short answer items in one section and all the multiple choice items in another.

Establish a format and instructions for each kind of item and be consistent in using this format. You may want to use the sample formats given in this chapter.

Occasionally you may want to use a open book test. This means that the students can use whatever textbook you specify as they answer the test questions. This doesn't test their ability to recall information, but it does require them to know how to look up and use specialized information when they need it.

Remember that any written test is a test of reading ability to some extent. Anyone who is not a good reader is at a disadvantage. Write test items carefully so that they are as easy to read as possible. Your goal is to find out how well your students know the subject; it is not to test their reading ability. Allow plenty of time so that slow readers can finish your test. If you have some who are very poor readers, you may want to make alternate plans for testing them.

CREATING A BANK OF TEST ITEMS

Once you've taken the time to put together a good test, you don't want to just use it once and scrap it. On the other hand, reusing the same test time after time has some serious pitfalls. For one thing, the same test may not quite fit each class you teach. Secondly, if a copy of the test gets out, it may get circulated and encourage cheating. Third, each time you give a test, you will probably find that some items need to be deleted or revised.

The trick is to save and reuse the items individually, rather than the test as a whole. By compiling a bank of test items that you can draw from, you can avoid writing each item from scratch each time you put together a new test. Use a computer word processing program if you can. If not, put each test item on a 3 x 5 card with the answer. When you are ready to make up a test, choose the items you need, and put them in the order you want. Then have the test typed up or printed out. The answer key for the test can also be typed up from the cards if they are kept in order.

Keeping a bank of test items on cards or computer has another big advantage—you can make notes. For example, if you decide a different working would be better, you can mark the change on the card or computer. You can record the date when that item was used in a test. This makes it easy for you to alternate items so that you don't use the same items for every test you give.

Not all test items are created equal. Some are better than others. You can use the cards or printout to record the results of an **item analysis**. This analysis, which you can do after you have graded a batch of tests, tells you how reliable each item is.

To do a item analysis, arrange the tests in order from the top score to the lowest score, and then make a record for each item of right and wrong answers (you can use X for correct and O for wrong).

Use this item analysis to judge how effective each item is. If most of the best students got the item right and most of the poorest got it wrong, it is probably a good item. On the other hand, if almost everyone got it right, or is almost everyone got it wrong, it is probably too easy or too hard. Occasionally you may find that the poor students got the item right and the good ones got it

Item Analysis

Test rank	Test score	Test items											
		1	2	3	4	5	6	7	8	9	10	12	13
1	79	x	O	x	x	x	x	O	x	x	x	x	x
2	87	x	O	x	x	x	x	x	O	x	x	O	x
3	82	x	O	x	x	x	x	x	x	x	x	x	x
4	75	x	O	O	x	x	x	O	x	x	x	O	x
5	78	O	O	x	x	O	x	x	O	O	x	O	x
6	70	x	x	x	O	x	O	O	x	x	O	x	O

x = Correct
O = Wrong

wrong. In that case, there may be something faulty in the way the item was written.

For example, in the partial item analysis above, item 2 needs to be examined. Most of the high scorers answered it incorrectly. If the low scorers answered it correctly, then the item is testing in reverse. Probably the more knowledgeable students are seeing something in the question that you did not mean to put there.

The results of the item analysis will help you improve your bank of test items. You may find out which kinds of items work best for you.

If you teach in a public school, a computer test service may be available to score a multiple choice test. If you have the students mark their answers on a special answer sheet, the computer will correct and score the test. It will also give you an item analysis. Check to see what services are available where you teach.

GUIDELINE FOR WRITTEN TESTS

Advance notice—Give notice of a written test well ahead of time so that the class can study for it. A test is a good way to motivate your class to review and study, but it only serves this purpose if they have time to study before the test. However, you may sometimes want to give a short quiz without warning as a way to make sure that they keep up with the class material.

Good test copy—Make sure the test copies that you give the class are clear and can be read easily. A test paper with poor format, misspellings, and other errors will slow and confuse the reader. The test you hand out should represent your craftsmanship as an instructor. If you are not confident about your ability to check your own spelling and grammar, you may want to have someone else proofread the test before you make copies for your class.

Content—Don't test for fussy details that may not be needed. Test for the fundamental knowledge and skills that the student needs to take from the class.

Format—Make sure that the format of each kind of test item is easy to use and easy to grade. Sample formats are shown in this chapter.

- **Don't have them put answers on a separate paper.** This can lead to confusion if they skip items or misnumber them. If the answers are on the test paper, you can see immediately which questions they are answering incorrectly. It is also much easier to use the test as a review when you hand it back if the answers are next to the questions.

- Have a space for the answer in a location so that it is easy for you to correct. Usually this means putting the answer lines at the left margin or the right margin. Avoid having them circle or underline the correct answer, because this format takes more time to check.

■ Have answer lines for a type of item all the same length so that the length of the answer line is not a clue to the correct answer. Make sure there is enough room for the answer.

■ Require only one answer for each numbered item. This makes calculating grades much easier. If you ask for three answers to one test item, you have to decide how to give credit if two answers are correct and one is wrong.

Simple wording—Keep the wording of the questions as simple and direct as possible. Cut out unnecessary words. If the sentences and questions in your test are long and involved, they may test reading ability instead of testing knowledge of the trade.

Careful wording—Try to make sure that the question cannot be misinterpreted. Read every test item you write carefully both when you write it and some time later when you can give it a fresh look

Trick questions—Avoid trick questions. They don't tell you who knows the material and who doesn't—they only tell you who noticed the trick you built into the question.

Challenges—Despite your best efforts, you may find that sometimes students will honestly misunderstand a question. Allow the class to challenge some test items, and if they have good reasons for objecting to certain questions, be willing to give in and allow alternate answers or not take credit off for the item. Remember that writing perfect test items is very difficult. Professional test-writing services spend many thousands of dollars writing, rewriting, and testing items for standardized tests, but they still have items challenged because they can cause misunderstanding. Such items may have to be removed from tests. Your class will respect you if you are reasonable and fair.

Instructions—Have written instructions so that the class knows how they are expected to answer the questions. Review the instructions with the class before they start the test so that they can ask questions if necessary.

Open book test—Occasionally you may want to give an open book test. This is not an invitation to cheat. It just means that the students can use whatever textbook you specify when they answer the test questions. An open book test does not test their ability to recall information. However, it does require them to know their book well and to know how to look up specialized information when they need it.

Timing—Time the test. Before they start the test, tell the class how much time they have to complete it. Five minutes before the end of the test, warn them of how much time they have left.

Supervise—Don't leave the room while they work on the test, and don't become so busy with your own work that you are not aware of what they are doing. You don't have to patrol the room like a prison guard, but neither do you have to issue them an open invitation to cheat.

Grading—Grade and return the test promptly, and review it with the class. Remember your purposes in giving the test. One reason for testing is to check your own teaching. If they have missed a large chunk of what you taught, you want to know that right away. Even more important, they need to know what they missed so they can correct any misunderstandings. They should do this while the test is still fresh in their minds. If you come back to it two or three weeks later, it's all old news and they will not be so concerned with the results.

TRUE/FALSE TEST

A true/false test often seems like the easiest kind of test to make up. However, writing a true/false test that really works is quite difficult. It is the weakest kind of test to use.

The main problem with a true/false test is that it makes guessing at the answers too easy. Someone can answer at random, without even looking at the questions, and easily get 50% of the answers right. You probably know from your own experience that someone who knows just a little bit about a subject can bluff and guess their way through a true/false test, unless the questions are very carefully written. But even a good true/false test can't really tell you if a student has mastered the subject, or just has a pretty good general idea.

It's also more difficult than it seems to write really good items that are entirely true or entirely false. Often true/false items in a test are not entirely clear-cut, and the class will want to argue about them.

You are better off avoiding true/false items in your tests.

MULTIPLE CHOICE TEST

A multiple choice test is easy to grade and can be used for most kinds of material. A sample format for multiple choice items is shown on the next page. The space for the answer is on the left margin to make the items easy to grade. A multiple choice test is a recognition test, since the correct answer only has to be recognized.

A typical multiple choice item gives a question or part of a statement and offers usually four choices to complete the statement or answer the question. In the sample on the opposite page, the second item asks a direct question. The first and third items are both partial statements that need to be completed with the correct choice.

Guidelines for Multiple Choice Test

There should be at least four possible answers. If there are only two or three, it's too easy to simply guess.

Each one of the choices should seem to be a reasonable answer that someone might choose. If the wrong answers are too obviously wrong, it will be too easy to guess the right answers.

MULTIPLE CHOICE

Put the letter of the correct answer in the blank.

_____ 1. When measuring initial flow rates for the terminals on a branch, the dampers
   A. should all be full closed.
   B. should all be full open.
   C. should all be half closed.
   D. can be in any position.

_____ 2. Which terminal is the most difficult to supply?
   A. The terminal with the lowest percentage of design flow
   B. The terminal with the highest percentage of design flow
   C. The terminal with the highest measured flow
   D. The last to be balanced

_____ 3. When some of the terminals in an air duct system are throttled down,
   A. the airflow rate and static pressure decrease.
   B. the airflow rate and static pressure increase.
   C. the airflow rate increases and the static pressure decreases.
   D. the airflow rate decreases and the static pressure increases.

Each one of the possible answers should fit the grammatical form of the partial sentence you set up. Read the partial sentence with each possible answer to make sure that it makes a good sentence.

Avoid grammatical clues. Don't end the partial sentence with *a* or *an* before the list of answers. That's an obvious clue as to which answer fits. Instead, put the required *a* or *an* with each of the four possible answers.

If you use a math problem, make all the answers within a reasonable range of the correct answer so that the student must make the calculation to determine the answer.

Make sure that the correct answers are spread equally between the four choices. In other words, don't set it up so that the second choice is always correct. Keep it random.

COMPLETION TEST

A completion test is a fill-in-the-blanks test. It requires the student to provide the word that completes a sentence. This tests recall, not just recognition, of the correct answer. This kind of test should usually call for a specific technical term to fit in the blank.

In the sample formats for completion items shown, notice that the space for the answer is on a separate answer line so that the length of the blank in the sentence is not a clue to the length of the answer. The answer line can go below the sentence, or it can be put at the left or right margin to make grading easy.

COMPLETION

In the blank to the left, write the word that best completes the sentence.

1._____ A magnetic field is created in the windings of the stator by _____.

2._____ Motors that need help to start their rotation are _____-phase motors.

COMPLETION

On the answer line below the sentence, write the word that best fits the blank.

3. A device that uses mechanical energy and converts it to electrical energy is a/an _____.

    _____

4. A device that uses electrical energy and converts it to mechanical energy is a/an _____ _____.

    _____

    _____

Guidelines for Completion Test

The word to be supplied should be a factual item **with no possibility of another wording that might fit**. For example, if you expect them to supply the word *larger*, some might choose another term, such as *bigger, greater,* or *more extensive*, which might be a valid answer. Then you have to decide whether or not it is correct. That makes it harder to grade and less objective.

Don't copy a sentence out of the textbook—that only checks the ability to remember the wording in the text. Put the sentence in your own words so that t is different from what the student has already read. This encourages real thinking about the item.

Use only one blank per sentence. Each blank should require just one word as the correct answer. If a blank is inserted in two places in the sentence, it's likely to cause confusion. However, sometimes a two-word phrase may be needed. In that case, there should be two blanks in the sentence and two blanks in the answer line. Item 4 on this page is an example of a two-word answer.

Word the sentence so that the blank is near the end of the sentence. This makes the sentence easier to read.

Make the blank in all completion items the same length. The length of the blank should not be a clue to the correct answer.

Don't have a or an alone before the blank, because this is a clue to the correct answer.

MATCHING TEST

A matching test tests recognition of the terms. A matching test is useful if there is a list of terms that are somewhat similar. It tests whether or not they know the difference between similar items.

A sample format for a matching test is shown below. The space for the letter of the correct answer is at the left margin. The items in the right-hand column are identified with letters. Do not have the students indicate answers by drawing a line between matching items because this is very difficult for you to grade.

MATCHING
Put the letter of the correct answer in the blank. Letters can be used more than once. Not all of the letters have to be used.

_____ 1. Kinetic energy

_____ 2. Thermal energy

_____ 3. Chemical energy

_____ 4. Electrical energy

_____ 5. Potential energy

A. The energy created in a dry cell battery

B. Energy that results from motion

C. Energy created by heat

D. Energy that can be released by splitting an atom

E. Energy that is often transmitted on copper wire

F. Stored energy

Guidelines for Matching Test

Usually a matching test should have no more than 10 or 15 items so that it isn't too hard to go through the list to choose from.

Generally you should put single words or short phrases in the column on the left. Put longer phrases—the definition or descriptions—in the column on the right.

Check your matching test carefully to make sure that only one answer fits each numbered item on the left. If you have designed the test so that answers from the right-hand column are correct for more than one item, put this information in the instructions.

It is a good idea to have more items in the column on the right than you need. Otherwise it's pretty easy to guess when the student gets to the last few. Just be sure that the instructions tell the class that not all of the items in the right-hand column are to be used.

The items in a matching test should be somewhat similar or related if possible. For example, they could be a list of tools. If all of the items are completely different, it is too easy to guess which matching item is correct.

Avoid giving away any obvious clues in the matching phrase.

IDENTIFICATION TEST

An identification test works well for testing the names of tools, parts of equipment, or other physical objects. It is generally used to test recall—the students are asked to identify the items, or drawings of the items. However, you can also use it as a recognition test if you give the list of terms you want and have your class match them up with the items to be identified. Sample formats for an identification test are shown on the next page. The first test is designed to check on recall. The second test is a recognition test because a list of the answers is given.

You can make up an identification test by photocopying **drawings** of items to identify. Photos do not photocopy well, so they should not be used.

IDENTIFICATION

In the blank write the name of the tool in the picture

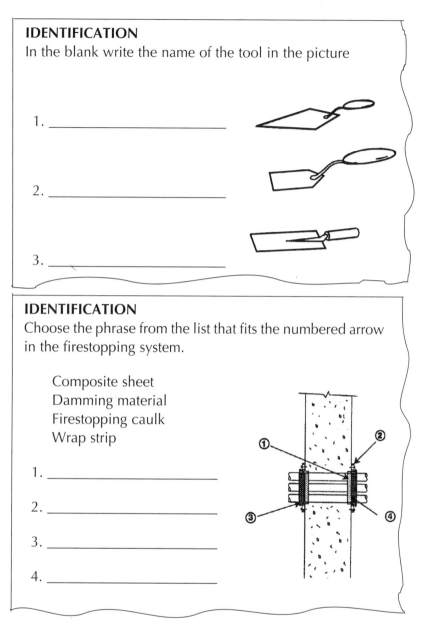

1. _____

2. _____

3. _____

IDENTIFICATION

Choose the phrase from the list that fits the numbered arrow in the firestopping system.

Composite sheet
Damming material
Firestopping caulk
Wrap strip

1. _____

2. _____

3. _____

4. _____

You can use an overhead projector to give an identification test to the whole class by showing numbered drawings and having them write down the answers. Make sure they number their answers correctly.

Probably the best kind of identification test is to have tools or equipment on display in the room with a number attached to each part you want them to identify. They can look at the actual item and write down the correct identification of each according to the number given.

Guidelines for Identification Test

If you use drawings, make sure they are clear and accurate.

If you have actual equipment for them to identify, make sure it is clear whether you are asking for the name of the whole piece of equipment of for the name of a part.

MATH TEST

The kind of math test you give should depend on the level of skill you expect your class to demonstrate. If you give them a group of calculations to do, you are only testing their ability to calculate. If you give them word problems that require them to solve a problem with math, you are testing whether they can apply math on the job.

A sample format for math problems is shown on the next page. If you want your class to show their calculations, allow enough space on the test page or have them use a separate page for a work sheet. Don't have them do their calculations on the back of the test page. For one thing, they are likely to make errors in copying the answer from the back of the sheet to the front. For another, you are less likely to use it to determine why they got a wrong answer if you have to turn the page back and forth from one side to another.

When you make up word problems, make them as realistic as possible. This is where your experience really counts. If you want to make your problems more challenging and more realistic, put in more information than they need to solve the problem—they will have to sort it out and select the facts and figures that they need to get to the answer.

MATH PROBLEMS

Calculate the area of the following. Give your answer in square feet to the nearest two decimal places. Show your calculations on this sheet.

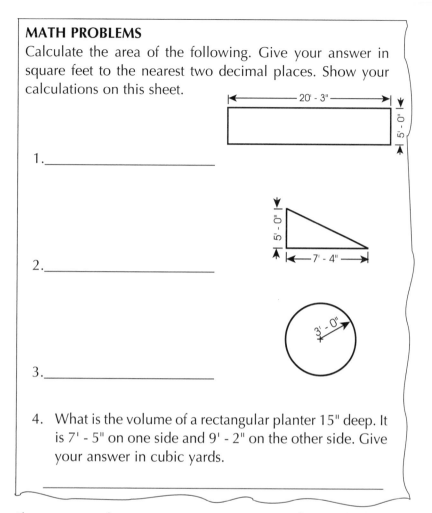

1._____

2._____

3._____

4. What is the volume of a rectangular planter 15" deep. It is 7' - 5" on one side and 9' - 2" on the other side. Give your answer in cubic yards.

_____

If you expect them to use an equation to make a calculation, decide whether they need to have the equation memorized, or whether they can look it up when it is required and only need to be able to use it when they have it. If you don't expect them to have the equation memorized, give them a list of equations along with the test items.

Guidelines for Math Test

Work all of the math problems yourself before you give them out to make sure they are appropriate, neither too easy nor too hard.

Double-check your answer key before you grade the test papers. It is very easy to get a wrong answer on your answer key. Use a calculator to check on yourself.

Specify the degree of accuracy you want in the answers. For example, specify that the answer should be to two decimal places, or the the nearest $\frac{1}{4}$ inch, or to the nearest dollar.

If you use math problems of varying difficulty, start with simpler problems and work up to more difficult ones.

When you write word problems, check them carefully to make sure you have included all the necessary information.

Decide whether calculators can be used.

SHORT ANSWER TEST

A short answer test requires a word or a phrase to answer a question. This is a recall test. Short answer questions seem to be easy to write, but they have to be written carefully. Usually you want to make sure that there is only one right answer. However, you may sometimes ask for an example, so a range of answers may be correct.

A sample format for a short answer test is shown on the next page. Note that the instructions for items 3 to 5 are given before the numbered answer lines.

Many of your students may be uncomfortable giving written answers. Reassure them. Let them know that these answers will be graded on content only, not on writing ability. Nevertheless, to some extent, any test that requires writing becomes a test of writing ability.

This type of test will be more objective if you ask for very short, specific answers. It may sometimes be useful to ask for a longer answer, such as explanation or a procedure. But if the answer

SHORT ANSWER

1. What kind of energy is the force of water stored behind a dam?

_____

2. A wagon is rolling downhill by itself. What kind of energy is this?

_____

Name three types of heat transfer and give an example of each:

3. _____

_____

4. _____

_____

5. _____

_____

given is poorly written, it may be difficult to decide if the answer is right or wrong. Therefore grading is subjective.

Guidelines for Short Answer Test

Provide more than enough space for the answer to allow for different styles of handwriting. Some students may need room so that they can cross out their first answer and replace it.

The amount of space left for the answer should not provide a clue to the answer. Leave the same amount of space for all the answers on this type of test.

Have only one answer for each numbered item. If you want them to provide a list of items, such as seven hand tools or four components, make each item in the list a separate numbered answer (See the sample format, items 3 to 5). If you ask for a list of five items for one answer, and three of the five are given correctly, it is difficult to decide how to score that item.

Ask your class to print clearly so that you can read their answers. You have to decide beforehand whether you will mark off for incorrect spelling. Your decision depends on the kind of class you are teaching.

ESSAY TEST

The dreaded essay test requires a paragraph or more to answer. Ideally, this type of test allows the student to show that they understand a complex procedure or know how to solve a problem that requires judgment. However, because many people find it difficult to explain their ideas in writing, an essay test can be a bad choice. If you teach a welding class, the goal is to teach skills and technical knowledge, not the ability to explain in writing.

On the other hand, if you are teaching a class of police officers who have to make reports, it is appropriate to have them write. Decide beforehand if you will grade your essay test for such things as organization, spelling, punctuation, or correct grammar. Let your students know what your standards are.

Before you grade the essay tests, make an answer key that lists the items or ideas that must be covered to earn an A grade. It will help you grade the papers and it will keep your grading more objective.

Guidelines for Essay Test

The question to be answered should be as specific as possible so that the class knows what kind of answer is expected.

The class should be given some time limits so that they know about how much time they have to answer.

SUMMARY

If you follow all the guidelines for writing test items, you should have a test that is fair and easy for you to grade. You'll have the right tool for the job. If you set up good standards and practices from the beginning, you will soon have a large bank of test items that you can use in many ways. That will make your teaching job much easier—and you'll feel confident that your testing and grading procedures are fair.

Chapter 9

GET THE PICTURE

USING OTHER MEDIA

A picture is worth a thousand words. That means that showing something is more useful than saying it. Of course the thing itself is worth ten thousand words. That means that handling something—a computer program, a new tool, a piping system, an electronic sensor—is more useful than seeing a picture of it.

But you can't always have the thing itself available. In that case a visual aid can be the next best way to show that item or to show how or why it is used or how it works. Visual media include overhead transparencies, DVDs, videos, slides, charts, models, boards, and flip charts. The most useful are transparencies, computer presentations, and DVDs. This chapter will explain how to use media effectively—and how to avoid potential problems.

One important reminder: sometimes a word is worth a thousand pictures. That means that some things cannot be shown—they have to be explained. Can you imagine conveying an idea of what you do on the job without using words? Even if you could show the **how** of it, you probably couldn't show the **why** or

when or many other fine points. Clearly teaching can't rely on visuals alone. You have to show AND tell.

COMPUTER PRESENTATIONS

Computer assisted presentations are widely used as a visual aid in teaching. **PowerPoint®** is the program most often used. Not only can you develop an effective slide presentation, but you can add such things as an outline, notes for your use, student handouts, and even overhead transparencies. The entire slide program is created on the computer, which allows many special effects such as color, different type fonts, special art or photos, sound, animation, and even short videos. Because they are stored in the computer, slides can easily be edited, changed, and placed in a different order. You can save your presentation on a CD or flash drive, so that you can run your presentation on other computers. Any computer that has Microsoft Office should be able to run a PowerPoint® presentation.

It takes time to learn the techniques of producing effective presentations with PowerPoint® and similar programs. Many tutorial programs are available on the Internet, and there are many books available on working with the PowerPoint® program.

In order to use PowerPoint® in your classroom, you need a laptop computer and a form of projection called an in-focus machine that connects to the computer. A screen is also required for projection. However, if you are working with only one to three students, they can read directly from the monitor. When using a PowerPoint® presentation, you press the *space bar* or *Enter* to move to the next slide. When you are finished with a slide but are not ready to move to the next one, press the "B" key. This "blackens" the screen, and avoids distraction from any classroom discussion. You can press the "B" key again to show the slide and proceed.

OVERHEAD TRANSPARENCIES
Overhead transparencies are 8½" x 11" clear plastic sheets on

which text and images are imprinted. They are placed on the light table of an overhead projector and projected onto a screen.

Transparencies are very easy to make. The plastic sheets are called **transparency film for plain paper copiers**. They can be purchased at any office supply store. Special sheets are also available for color printers and for computer-created art produced on laser printers. Any material that can be photocopied can be copied onto the transparency film. The finished transparencies can be taped onto cardboard mounting frames or stored in protective plastic sleeves. Both of these items can be purchased at any office supply store. Plastic sleeves are less bulky. However the mounting frames provide a border for the transparency and block out distracting light. They also prevent the transparency from curling.

Even though overhead transparencies are an older process, they still have many advantages:

- The equipment is very simple so there is little chance of crashing in the middle of a presentation. About the only thing that can go wrong is a burned-out projection bulb.

- Projection equipment is relatively cheap. Usually you can have a projector in your classroom at all times.

- The ease of producing transparencies and the simplicity of the equipment makes it more likely that you will use visual aids in your teaching.

Overlays

Overlays are additional transparencies that can be added to or removed from the base transparency. They are aligned to fit with the base transparency material. Overlays are usually hinged with tape to the mounting frame. This allows them to immediately fall into the proper position with the base transparency without any shuffling. Hinging also assures that the overlays will not be misplaced or shown in the wrong order. They can be added or removed from the base drawing as desired. They are useful for such things as showing the progressive build-up of an item or the stages of a procedure. Use them to add names or numbers to a drawing. Use overlays to avoid putting too much material on one transparency at a time.

Overlays that must be shown in a specific order are all hinged on the same side of the frame. Overlays that may be shown in different orders are hinged on different sides of the frame.

Overlays are useful to help you teach the names of different items. For example, use overlays to test for tool names. The base can have drawings of different tools. An overlay can have numbers that go under each tool. You can ask students to name each numbered tool. Then you can use a second overlay to place the name under each tool.

If you put blank overlay over a base drawing, you can use it to draw or write on with washable markers. (Special fine-point overlay markers are available) Markers are useful to add color, write labels, or add suggestions from students during a discussion. Marks from washable markers can be removed with a moist tissue. Using a blank overlay protects your base transparency from damage.

USING PowerPoint® AND TRANSPARENCIES

Both computer presentations and overhead transparencies have an advantage over DVDs and videos—it is easier to maintain an instructional mode. The classroom can and should be lighted, although the lighting should be dim enough, especially near the screen, so that the presentations is clear. Also, you are in the front of the room, facing the class. This allows you to judge student reactions, ask questions, and start discussions. It is also easier for students to take notes—which helps maintain an active learning situation.

But both PowerPoint® and transparencies have two areas where you must use skill to create a successful program:

- **Designing** the material
- **Teaching** the material

Designing Computer Slides and Transparencies

The **design** of computer slides or transparencies can either promote learning or detract from learning. Design includes the size and style of print, the amount of text, and the use of color and art. Much of this depends upon your own judgment and ability. However I have listed below some of the important things you should keep in mind:

- **Your goal is to educate**. Be careful to avoid "PowerPointitis." Computer presentation programs are so versatile that it is easy to get carried away with special effects and other gimmicks that actually distract from the educational message. When you complete your presentation, examine each slide or transparency critically. Does it contribute to the objectives of your lesson plan—or is it just fluff?

- The message on a slide or transparency must be brief. A general rule is to have no more than seven lines of text and seven words per line. Emphasize important ideas, basic principles, key points. Each display should be the starting point upon which you expand your ideas, tell your experiences, ask questions, and start discussions.

- Each display is a visual outline. Show short statements, graphs, charts, or tables that you can talk about.

- Keep it simple and uncluttered. Any chart, graph, or table should be clear and easy to grasp. Try to avoid any text that runs vertically instead of horizontally.

- Combine text with images where possible. "A picture is worth a thousand words."

- Use color and bullets to emphasize the points you want to make.

- Use white space to set off blocks of text. Do not fill the whole slide. Keep them easy to read, see, and quickly comprehend.

- Use type sizes that can easily be read at any point in the room. Try standing in key points in your room to be sure you can read the text. In general, anything smaller than an 18 point font is suspect. For overhead transparencies, avoid photocopying text from books or magazines. It is almost always too wordy and too small. Use your computer to reword the text and to produce it in a suitable size.

- There the many web sites where you can download images, called clip art. Use clip art sparingly. Everyone else is using it too.

- Have fun. Be creative.

- Be sure to make all your revisions to your PowerPoint® program before you save it onto a CD or flash drive to use on another computer.

Teaching with Slides and Transparencies

Slides and transparencies are not teachers and don't give you a vacation from teaching. They are just useful tools for you, the instructor. You are the learning manager. Before you develop the presentation, you should have a lesson plan using the Four Steps of Instruction. Don't forget to include the Application and Test steps. Use questions, discussions, and related problems to keep the students actively involved in the learning process.

Use the following techniques to make your teaching more effective:

- Run and rehearse your presentation before you use it in class.

- Set up and try your equipment and presentation before class. View the screen from all parts of the room.

- Set up the screen where it is best seen by all students. For transparencies, this is generally in the front corner of the room. If you are right handed, the projector should be at your right hand when you are facing the class.

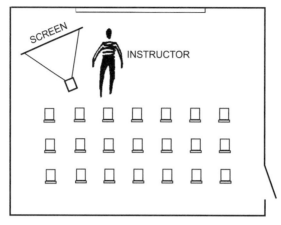

The right room arrangement allows you to face the class while you use transparencies

■ It is wise to have back-up transparencies or handouts from your PowerPoint® presentation in case your computer crashes or you have technical problems with the equipment.

■ Usually the projector is below the center of the screen. This results in **keystoning**—the image will be wider at the top of the screen than on the bottom. If the screen can be tilted out at the top, keystoning can be eliminated.

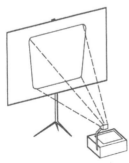

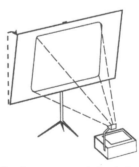

Keystoning causes a distorted image on the screen

Tilting the screen corrects keystoning

- Don't read the slides aloud. Pause with each new slide and allow your students to read the information or at least take in the data on the slide first. Your job is to do such things as expand the ideas, give detailed explanations, add your experiences, ask questions, and pose problems related to the material.

- Talk to the students—not to the screen.

- Don't get tied to where computer or overhead table is. Be sure to move around the front of the classroom to continue to engage all the students and make the teaching more interesting.

- Don't rush. Give your audience time to absorb the ideas you are presenting. Your added input should take at least two minutes for each screen display.

- It is too awkward to try to point to items on the screen. For PowerPoint®, use a laser pointer judiciously. A common mistake is to overuse a laser pointer, making it a distraction instead of a help. Put the pointer down when not using it so you don't fiddle with it. For overhead transparencies, use a slim pointer or a pencil at the transparency, not at the screen.

Organize Your Visuals

As with all your teaching material, keep visuals filed so that you can find them next year. Be sure that your lesson plan lists all the visuals you will need.

Give computer presentations a file name with the lesson number and name. For overhead transparencies, number each frame in the order that they are to be shown and file them in a folder under the lesson number.

DVDs and VIDEOS

At their best, DVDs and videos give you the best of both worlds. By using both words and images, they **show** and **tell**. They can also show things that cannot be presented in any other way. Used carefully and occasionally they can be valuable teaching aids. But there are also many pitfalls in their use.

Teachers too often have used a DVD or a video as a vacation from teaching. It's a strong temptation. Why not put on a video and let all those professionals with high-tech backup take over your class for a while?

When a DVD or video comes on, some students expect entertainment. Others simply expect to be bored. Either way, many students will automatically tune out learning when they come on. Even those who want to learn may let their minds drift. Most follow what's on the screen in a general way without paying close attention to details.

The problem is clear—when students watch a video, they are just passive learners. Your challenge is to make a video part of an active learning experience.

First of all, make sure the video definitely belongs with your lesson. Titles, summaries, and recommendations can be very misleading. Before you consider using a video, view it yourself. Don't use a video that doesn't fit your lesson.

If you decide the video is right for your lesson, the next step is to watch it again. Review the video carefully to determine exactly **how** you can use it. Make notes on the key points covered. Plan where you can stop it while you ask questions and discuss the content of part of the video. Make a list of questions to ask or other activities to coordinate with the video.

When you bring the video to class, don't just plug it in and turn it on. Introduce it. Tell your students what they will be viewing, how it ties in with the course, and, most important, what they should watch for.

Watch it again—this time with your class. Never leave the room. That tells the class you are using the video as a babysitter. While you are watching with them you can keep them focused on the information you want them to get from the video. You can pause the video at appropriate times to ask questions or to add your own comments.

When the video is finished, don't just drop it and go on to something else. Keep the subject alive with questions, comments, and discussion related to the viewing. Make sure the class sees the connection between the video and the rest of the lesson.

In short, do everything you can to get the class actively involved so that they really pay attention to the video. Don't just turn it on and tune them out.

CHARTS, MODELS, AND OTHER VISUALS

Manufacturers of products used in your field may have visual aids that you can use in your classes. These could be charts, material samples, models (whole or cut-away) and the like. You might be able to use a poster showing a cut-away view of a pump. You might get a display of various roofing materials. You might use a chart of computer program commands.

Talk to manufacturers' representatives in your area. Many of them will be glad to help obtain teaching materials.

However, just posting these visual aids in your classroom doesn't mean that they will promote learning. Remember that students have to be actively involved in learning. As always, that's something you control as a learning manager. Work the visual aids into your lesson plan. Have a student identify parts of a model or drawing. Ask questions about how to use an informational chart, or have them identify material samples as part of a quiz or test.

BOARDS AND FLIP CHARTS

Whether you use chalkboards, marker boards, or flip charts, the teaching techniques are the same. However, the tools are slightly different:

- **Chalkboards** are black or a light color—often a light green. The writing material is chalk. White chalk is most common, but colored chalks are also available.

- **Marker boards** (also called **white boards**) have a white, glossy surface that will not take chalk. A special dry-erase marker is used. These are available in many colors. They can be erased in the same way as a chalkboard. A warning: Don't store permanent markers close to dry-erase markers. If a permanent marker is used by mistake on a marker board, the marks have to be removed with a cleaning fluid.

- **Flip charts** are pads of 25" x 30" sheets of paper that can be removed from the pad when filled. Often they are fastened to the wall so that they can be referred to as a discussion develops. Pads are available with adhesive strips so they can be fastened to a wall without pins or tape. Any marker will work on flip chart sheets, but the best results are from special flip chart markers. They are designed to flow well when used on vertical surfaces and they will not bleed through the paper or smudge.

Teaching Methods

As you teach, you will likely learn (as I have) of some excellent board techniques. Include the use of boards and flip charts in your lesson plans. They can be used in all of the Four Steps of Instruction—for example:

- INTRODUCTION—Add words, phrases, or sketches and ask students if they know their significance.

- PRESENTATION—Clarify parts of your presentation by writing math problems, sketching wiring diagrams, or jotting notes of important points of a lecture or discussion.

- APPLICATION—Have students solve a math problem, finish a sketch, or write the steps of a process.

- TEST—Use for an informal quiz by writing math problems for them to solve, or by drawing geometric shapes or other items for them to identify.

Be organized and clear when you use a board or flip chart. Plan ahead about how you are going to use the board or chart. The more organized your board presentation is, the more students will absorb:

- Don't just scribble in a hodgepodge of words and phrases.

- If you are using major headings as an outline of your material, leave enough room to add material under each heading.

- View your material from the back of the room to see if it can be easily read and easily understood.

Don't talk to the board. Stop talking while you are writing and your back is to the room. Then turn and face the class to continue your comments and ask questions. If you draw on the board and speak at the same time, the class will get distracted and lose interest.

Get your students involved. More learning happens when students are actively involved. Have students do such things as:

- Finish a math problem.

- Demonstrate a process, such as how to bisect an angle; how to wire a switch and light fixtures; or how to develop the pattern for a sheet metal funnel.

- Write the major points of a discussion on the board.

- Use the board or flip chart as part of any reports they give to the class.

SUMMARY

Various media can add visual impact to your lessons or they can be a disaster. The difference is in how well you use them. They can't do the teaching for you. You have to keep control.

PowerPoint® or transparencies allow you to keep control of the class more effectively than other media. They are a great way to get the class actively involved in learning.

DVDs and videos can lull your class into a passive mode. If you use them, you have to be careful to keep the class alert and actively involved through the use of questions, discussion, and other activities.

Charts, material samples, models, and other visuals are useful if you coordinate them with the rest of your lessons. Just showing them isn't enough—you have to USE them.

Whatever you do, stay in control. You are the learning manager. Your students can learn a lot from you. But they won't learn if you don't TEACH!

FINAL NOTE

It's up to you now.

If you have already been teaching for a while, I hope this book helps you iron out some wrinkles.

If you are new to teaching, you may face the prospect with reservations. You might be surprised. Many of us get into teaching kicking and dragging our feet and then find out we like it. There is an excitement to passing on your knowledge to others who are eager to learn—and you will probably find that your students are eager.

Now get out there and *Teach!*

Index

E

Essay test, 124-125
Evaluation standards, 64-65

F

Flip charts, *See* Boards and flip charts
Four steps of instruction, 16-26
Frequent successes, 10-11

G

Goals, 5
Grade records, 67-69
Grading, 101-104
Guest speakers, 34-35, 46-47

H

Housekeeping, 71-72

I

Identification test, 118-120
Individual instruction, 53-54
Individual pace, 8-9
Introduction step, 17-18, 22-25, 87-88, 136

J

Job sheets, 62-63

K

Key questions, 64

L

Learning manager, 27-36
Lecture, 42-46

R

S

T

U